# THE MONARCH EFFECT

## SURVIVING POISON, PREDATORS, AND PEOPLE

### DANA L. CHURCH

SCHOLASTIC
FOCUS
NEW YORK, NY

All rights reserved. Published by Scholastic Focus, an imprint of Scholastic Inc.,
*Publishers since 1920.* SCHOLASTIC, SCHOLASTIC FOCUS, and associated logos are
trademarks and/or registered trademarks of Scholastic Inc.

The publisher does not have any control over and does not assume any
responsibility for author or third-party websites or their content.

Library of Congress Cataloging-in-Publication Data available
ISBN 978-1-338-74922-9

10 9 8 7 6 5 4 3 2 1        24 25 26 27 28

Printed in Italy    183
First edition, April 2024

Book design by Maeve Norton and Emily Muschinske

*For Stacey,*
*who said, "Butterflies . . ."*
*And for Dad—*
*I wish you could have read this one, too.*

This book was written on the traditional land of the Anishinaabe, Haudenosaunee, and Neutral peoples, and I respectfully acknowledge their Ancestors and Elders, past and present, and the generations to come. As readers, we may be gathering on other traditional lands from around the world, and I honor the enduring presence and deep traditional knowledge, laws, and philosophies of the Indigenous people with whom we all share these lands today.

—Dana L. Church

# TABLE OF CONTENTS

# RIVERS OF BUTTERFLIES

Years ago, a boy named Homero Aridjis lived in the village of Contepec, in the State of Michoacán, a few hours northwest of Mexico City. Each winter, Aridjis and other villagers gazed up in awe as waves of thousands of monarch butterflies streamed through the air. He said it looked like his village was filled with "aerial rivers" of orange-and-black butterflies.

The residents of Contepec knew that between November and March each year, monarch butterflies made their homes in the nearby **oyamel fir trees**. The butterflies would swoop down from the forest on Altamirano Hill, flying through the village streets in search of water. "When I was at school," recalled Aridjis, "we went as an excursion every year to the sanctuaries in the mountain called Cerro Altamirano. Then it was like the excursion of the year for us as children to see the butterflies in the sanctuaries."

Can you imagine seeing thousands of monarch butterflies flying through the streets in your town or city? This was in the 1940s, before scientists knew much about monarch butterflies. The sanctuaries Aridjis visited as a child were unknown to people outside Mexico. Since then, things have changed. Today, monarch butterflies are famous around the globe. Each year, tourists from all over visit the monarch butterfly sanctuaries. Scientists now have a much better understanding of these "winged tigers," as Aridjis called them. Recently, this iconic butterfly was classified as vulnerable to extinction on the International Union for Conservation of Nature (IUCN) Red List of Threatened Species. The quest to understand monarch butterflies—and to save them—is a story as colorful as the butterflies themselves. There has been collaboration and conflict, colonialism and conservation, experiments and surprises. And there is still an abundance of mystery. Let's venture into the wild and wonderful world of monarch butterflies.

## CHAPTER ONE

# BABY MONARCHS AND BARFING BLUE JAYS

A little egg, barely the size of a pinhead, sits on the underside of a milkweed leaf. After four to five days, if you were to look at the egg through a magnifying glass, you would see that the top of the egg has turned black. That's the head of the baby monarch caterpillar that's inside, and it's ready to come out.

Once the tiny, pale green caterpillar with its shiny black head breaks through the eggshell, it eats the shell. The eggshell, known as the **chorion**, is mostly protein, and this makes for a nutritious first meal for the caterpillar. And the pale green caterpillar must eat in order to grow, because it is barely as big as the writing on a dime.

After the tiny caterpillar has eaten all of its eggshell, it's ready to eat even more. Luckily, the milkweed leaf it's on provides a feast. However, the caterpillar can't dig in just yet. The surface of the leaf is covered in hairs called **trichomes**. When you're as small as a newly hatched monarch caterpillar, those hairs are like big spikes. The caterpillar sets to work, cutting the trichomes with its mouth. It

FIGURE 1-1. Close-up view of a monarch egg on the underside of a milkweed leaf.

doesn't eat the trichomes, but instead acts sort of like a mini lawn mower.

Once the caterpillar has cleared a spot, it still can't chomp down on the leaf. It must bite with care, because under the surface of the milkweed leaf are special cells that contain a white, oozing liquid called **latex**. When the caterpillar bites down and punctures these cells, the latex immediately spurts out and is extremely sticky. It also dries fast like glue, so the caterpillar risks getting its mouth stuck shut or even its body stuck on the leaf, unable to move. On top of that, the latex is filled with deadly poisons. Scientist Dr. Anurag Agrawal described the monarch caterpillar's situation like this: "Visualize a toddler trying to eat a salad, with lettuce leaves covered in cactus spikes and with a dressing made of thick and toxic glue." What a challenge for the poor hungry caterpillar!

But let's look at things from the milkweed's point of view. Monarch caterpillars eat these plants. The plants need to defend themselves, so they developed trichomes and latex. As we will see, milkweed also developed special poisons. Sometimes that poison can kill monarch caterpillars; other times the caterpillars are able to use it to their advantage. If that wasn't enough, milkweed plants also give off smells that attract predators, such as wasps, flies, spiders, and stinkbugs, that would gladly make a monarch caterpillar their next meal. How does a newly hatched caterpillar deal with all this? When it comes to predators that hunt them down, the caterpillar unfortunately has no defenses yet and they often end up dying.

But if a caterpillar is not found by another hungry critter, it has to deal with the gush of latex from the milkweed leaf it will encounter when it bites the leaf.

**FIGURE 1-2.** Some types of milkweed are woollier than others. Top: Monarch caterpillars of different ages on less-woolly milkweed leaves. Bottom: A monarch caterpillar on a milkweed leaf with lots of trichomes.

Do caterpillars have a strategy to deal with the sticky goo? Here is what scientists know about what caterpillars typically do on common milkweed (*Asclepias syriaca*). First, the caterpillar takes a bite out of the leaf. Then it backs away, wiping any latex that got onto its head or legs onto the leaf. It eventually returns to where it bit the leaf and bites again. It slowly chews a moat around itself, creating a little island where it can feed.

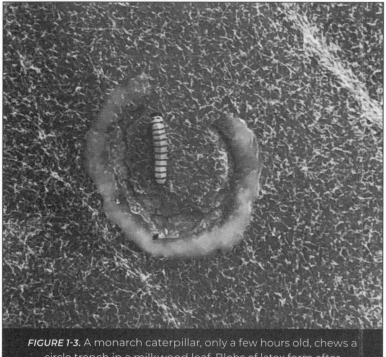

**FIGURE 1-3.** A monarch caterpillar, only a few hours old, chews a circle trench in a milkweed leaf. Blobs of latex form after the caterpillar bites the leaf.

Dr. Agrawal calls this a "circle trench." Sometimes the caterpillars will dig the circle trench at the same time as they shave off the trichomes, while other times they shave off the trichomes in a circle first.

Less than half of all monarch caterpillars survive the milkweed's latex. That's an incredible number of caterpillars that die, considering one female monarch butterfly lays several hundred eggs in her lifetime. This means latex is quite an effective way for the milkweed to defend itself from being eaten alive. If the amount of latex a caterpillar ends up accidentally eating doesn't kill them, they can recover in five to ten minutes. Otherwise, they end up in a nonresponsive, coma-like state and die.

Newly hatched caterpillars face various challenges, depending on the type of milkweed plant their mother laid their egg on. If a caterpillar was lucky enough to be laid on butterfly weed (*Asclepias tuberosa*), which can be found across North America, and is a type of milkweed that produces little if any latex, the baby caterpillar can dive right in without having to make a circle trench. On the other hand, if a baby caterpillar finds itself on sandhill milkweed (*Asclepias humistrata*), which is quite common in Florida, it has to deal with a very waxy, slippery surface. Caterpillars can easily fall off to their death (another way that the milkweed plant defends itself from being eaten). Sandhill milkweed also produces lots of latex. Caterpillars born on this type of milkweed have their work cut out for them. To deal with the slipperiness and all the latex, monarch caterpillars on sandhill milkweed spin a thick mat of silk that acts as a platform where they can rest and not fall off the leaf. It also helps stop the flow of latex once the caterpillar starts chewing the leaf. A pretty clever strategy, if you ask me.

It is amazing that a creature so small has different survival strategies, depending on the type of milkweed plant it finds itself on. To test this even further, scientists took monarch butterfly eggs from common milkweed in New York and placed them on sandhill milkweed in Florida. They also did the reverse: They took monarch eggs laid on sandhill milkweed in Florida and placed them on common milkweed leaves in New York. The result? The New Yorker caterpillars started spinning silk mats in Florida, and the Floridian caterpillars started digging circle trenches in New York. The caterpillars adjusted their behavior depending on the circumstances they found themselves in. Amazing!

If a monarch caterpillar survives past its first few days of life, its next job is to eat, eat, and eat some more. Caterpillars are basically eating, growing, and pooping machines. It takes about a week for a monarch caterpillar to grow from being barely the size of the writing on a dime to about the size of a sunflower seed. Although that is still quite small, it is a big difference in size. The caterpillar keeps growing until it reaches between one to one and a half inches, a little bit smaller than the length of your thumb. Dr. Agrawal put the caterpillar's growth spurts in perspective: "If an eight-pound human baby were to grow at this rate, by the end of one year, she would weigh as much as thirty-five of the largest adult elephants, about half a million pounds."

One funny thing about all this growing is that a caterpillar's skin doesn't grow with it. Imagine not being able to change into larger clothes as you grow bigger. You would eventually burst out of your clothes! This is essentially what happens to monarch caterpillars: They burst out of their skin. There is a soft, new skin underneath that quickly hardens. This bursting, or shedding of skin, is called **molting**. Monarch caterpillars molt five times before forming a **chrysalis** (a protective covering). The space of time between each molt is called an **instar**. So, monarch caterpillars go through five instars before turning into an adult butterfly. Often the caterpillar will eat its old, discarded skin. Yuck! I can't imagine eating my old, discarded clothes, let alone my own skin!

Milkweed leaves don't contain much nutrition, so monarch caterpillars have to eat a lot of leaves to get the energy and nutrients they need to grow. This is pretty much the case for all **herbivores**, or animals that eat plants. This is the opposite of **carnivores**, or animals that eat meat. Meat is very dense in nutrients and so the animal doesn't have to eat nearly as much or as often to get similar benefits. For example, a panda bear needs to eat up to eighty-four pounds of bamboo leaves each day to stay healthy, whereas a lion eats about an average of seventeen to twenty pounds of meat per day. Monarch caterpillars eat so much that if you were to look inside their body, it would be entirely filled with ground-up milkweed leaves. And most of the leaf material can't be digested, so monarch caterpillars poop . . . a lot (see Figure 1-4).

Although monarch caterpillars are little eating machines, they do have one other important job: to not be eaten! How do they defend themselves against the flies and wasps that try to make them their meal? Interestingly, monarch caterpillars react to sounds, and they react to the buzzing of a predator's wings as it approaches. The

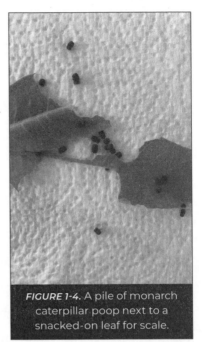

FIGURE 1-4. A pile of monarch caterpillar poop next to a snacked-on leaf for scale.

caterpillar freezes, ducks, or twitches its head up and down, waves the two antennae-like filaments on its head (called **tentacles**), or even drops off the plant. Freezing is thought to be helpful because some insect predators can zero in on their prey only if it is moving. Ducking, twitching, or waving their head shoos the predator away, and dropping off the plant is a quick escape. Scientists have seen these responses by monarch caterpillars when the scientists play recordings of buzzing insect wings and when bumble bees (who don't eat caterpillars) fly nearby. Monarch caterpillars also respond to human voices and even to jets. This was a surprise finding by two scientists, Dame Miriam Rothschild and Dr. Gunnar Bergström, who wrote:

> Once or twice weekly, these machines [Harrier aircrafts] sweep across the greenhouse, the pilots from the local base thus exhibiting their skill in low flying exercises. The loud aerial disturbance frightens the human bystanders if unaccustomed to the sudden rushing noise; and the vibration not infrequently cracks panes of glass in the roof of the greenhouse. The caterpillars, in unison, are then thrown into violent paroxysms of head jerking and tentacle waving, which subsides equally suddenly as the jets vanish. The effect is striking, occasionally on-lookers burst out laughing as the food plant appears momentarily to have come alive!

If monarch caterpillars can hear all these sounds, do they have ears? Not exactly. Scientists found very tiny hairs near the caterpillar's head that are connected to nerve cells. When these hairs were removed, the caterpillars stopped reacting to sounds. What might the experience of sound be like for a caterpillar? That remains a secret.

## NATURE'S FASHION STATEMENT

One other peculiar thing about monarch caterpillars is how brightly colored they are, with their white, black, and yellow stripes. Scientists aren't sure whether **invertebrate** predators (animals without a backbone) can see the bright advertisement of a monarch caterpillar's presence. However, **vertebrates** (animals with a backbone), such as birds, certainly can. And birds are another predator that monarch caterpillars have to watch out for. Does the monarch caterpillar's brightly colored body attract birds, and as a result, are they eaten more often than other types of caterpillars that blend in with their surroundings?

Dr. Colleen Hitchcock did a clever experiment that helps us answer this question. She made life-size clay models of caterpillars: Some were green that blended in with leaves, some were the same shade of brown as branches, and the rest were white with painted yellow-and-black stripes, just like monarch caterpillars. Dr. Hitchcock then placed these clay caterpillars on branches and leaves all over the fields and forests of Moose Hill Wildlife

Sanctuary and Assabet River National Wildlife Refuge in eastern Massachusetts. To prevent birds from flying off with the clay models, she tied the models to the branches or leaves with clear nylon thread. Before placing all her clay caterpillars out in the field, though, she made sure that caterpillars and birds already naturally existed in the areas. She found hundreds of green caterpillars, brown caterpillars, and monarch caterpillars, as well as over sixty species of birds. The most common birds she encountered were blue jays, American crows, tree swallows, black-capped chickadees, American robins, gray catbirds, northern mockingbirds, eastern towhees, northern cardinals, and American goldfinches. Would these birds be fooled by her clay models?

Altogether, Dr. Hitchcock made and used over 3,000 clay caterpillars. She put them in the field for twenty-one days and checked on each one every three days. She was looking for beak marks left by birds when they pecked at them. Dr. Hitchcock was clever and used a type of clay that didn't harden. Beak marks were V-shaped patterns in the clay or pairs of angled marks. She counted how many clay caterpillars had these attack marks on them and noted the color of these attacked clay caterpillars.

Over 600 clay caterpillars were attacked by birds. This was roughly 21 percent of the total number of clay caterpillars Dr. Hitchcock had placed out in the field. Therefore, many birds were fooled into thinking they were real caterpillars. Interestingly, the monarch clay models were attacked way less often and "survived" much longer compared with the green and brown caterpillars. This is a curious and very important finding. Monarch caterpillars are much easier to see, so you'd think they would have been attacked by birds much sooner and more often compared to the camouflaged green or brown models that blended in with their surroundings. It was as though birds were avoiding the clay monarch caterpillars. Why would that be?

Let's go back to milkweed for a moment. Milkweed is filled with poisons called **cardenolides**. Cardenolides are found in the roots, leaves, latex, seeds, and **nectar** of milkweed plants. Most animals, including humans, become sick and even die from eating cardenolides. Thanks to a single DNA[1] mutation, monarchs can tolerate doses thousands of times higher than what the human body can stand. When monarch caterpillars

---

1. DNA stands for deoxyribonucleic acid. DNA is found in cells, and it is like a microscopic bead on a string that contains the instructions or recipe for how to build a living thing.

eat the cardenolides that are in milkweed leaves, their tiny bodies store the poisons. By storing the poisons (a process called **sequestration**), the monarch caterpillar becomes poisonous itself, which protects it from predators such as birds. The monarch caterpillar's bright yellow, black, and white coloring acts as a warning: "Eat me and you'll be poisoned!"

**IT'S TRANSFORMATION TIME!**
When a monarch caterpillar is about two weeks old, it stops its milkweed leaf binge. No longer interested in eating, it enters into its "wandering phase." It crawls away from the milkweed plant where it hatched and was feeding upon, and searches for a place to **pupate**: to form a chrysalis and transform into a butterfly. The best place to pupate is sheltered from the wind and rain. Scientists believe the wandering phase allows the monarch caterpillar to leave all its "evidence" behind, such as chewed leaves and **frass** (poop), so that predators can't easily find its soon-to-be-constructed chrysalis.

Before the monarch caterpillar pupates, it has one last poop to remove any remaining food waste in its gut. The caterpillar finds a sturdy place, such as a branch, and it spins a silk button. It then hangs upside down from this button in a J-shape. Then comes its final molt. Its skin splits open one last time and underneath is the pale green **pupa** (the stage between a caterpillar and a butterfly). The pupa spins and twirls in a "pupa dance," and when it is finished, it is covered with a beautiful jade-green chrysalis with a gold trim.

Over the next one to two weeks, the jade-and-gold chrysalis hangs in silence. But inside, something spectacular happens. Scientists call it **metamorphosis**. The caterpillar transforms from its wormlike body into a winged butterfly. What an amazing feat, considering how different caterpillars and butterflies are!

How does it work? What goes on inside the chrysalis? Much of the process is still a mystery. The caterpillar dissolves into a soupy liquid, and then its cells somehow are rearranged into a butterfly. This transformation takes about seven to ten days. One group of scientists wanted to learn more, so they used **magnetic resonance imaging (MRI)** to look inside the chrysalises of monarch pupae during metamorphosis. MRI is normally used in the medical field: It's a big machine that takes pictures of the inside of our bodies so that we can see bones, internal organs, and other tissues. MRI allowed the scientists to take lots of pictures of the inside of chrysalises as the pupae were changing into adult butterflies. What did they see?

When they compared MRI pictures of a new, one-day-old chrysalis to a ten-day-old chrysalis (when the butterfly was ready to come out), they found that the caterpillar's digestive tract had transformed into internal body parts that the adult butterfly will need: flight muscles, tubes for delivering air to the muscles, and reproductive organs. They could not see any wings by the fourth day, but by day six, wings were clearly visible inside the chrysalis. Interestingly, the scientists could see the caterpillar's eyes, but not its brain, on the first day inside the chrysalis. The scientists wrote, "Even though the caterpillar seems to lose its head when it sheds its skin, its eyes remain within the chrysalis and they become the butterfly's eyes." The caterpillar's heart, which is a long tube with pumps along the length of the inside of the caterpillar's body, continues to beat during metamorphosis, although there are some spaces of time during early butterfly development when it is silent. It starts beating again continuously when the adult butterfly is getting ready to emerge. The heart stays intact throughout all the changes, but it becomes thinner, longer, and denser in the new butterfly. Perhaps as technology improves over time, we can learn even more details about how exactly caterpillars turn into butterflies.

About twenty-four hours before the monarch butterfly is ready to emerge, the chrysalis turns from jade green to transparent, and you can see the new monarch butterfly folded up inside. When the butterfly is ready to come out, it pushes its way through the chrysalis, splitting it open. Once the new butterfly is fully out of the chrysalis, it hangs out for a while. One of the first things it does is uncurl its long, tubelike tongue, called a **proboscis**, and sticks it out. Scientists are not sure why it does this. As a caterpillar, the monarch butterfly didn't have a long proboscis, so maybe it feels different and the butterfly is stretching it and trying it out.

The wings of the new monarch butterfly are crumpled and damp. While the butterfly hangs out, it pumps body fluid through the veins of its wings to make them flatten and stiffen. It is important at this stage that nothing touches the new wings—otherwise, they might not form properly. In less than half an hour, the butterfly's wings will be fully expanded and dry. But the butterfly will rest for a few hours before its first flight.

## BARFING BLUE JAYS

What about all those poisonous cardenolides that the caterpillar ate from milkweed leaves? It turns out the cardenolides move through the chrysalis during metamorphosis and end up in the adult butterfly's wings. Specifically, they end up highly concentrated in the wing scales. Butterfly wings are made up of tiny scales that, if you gently rub the wings between your thumb and index finger, come off as a kind of powder-looking substance. Concentrating the cardenolides in the wing scales is a very smart strategy for two reasons: (1) the poisons are far away from the butterfly's own internal organs, and (2) predators, such as birds, usually grab the butterfly by its wings. When the predator seizes the wings, it can inhale or taste the bitter wing scales. It would drop the butterfly, and the butterfly would have a pretty good chance of surviving. The predator, on the other hand, would remember the nasty-tasting experience and probably never try to eat a monarch again.

The consequences of eating a monarch butterfly were clearly shown by Dr. Lincoln Brower and Dr. Jane Van Zandt Brower. They were scientists and a husband-and-wife team who are famous for their "barfing blue jay project." Back in the 1950s, the Browers kept a bunch of monarch caterpillars in their lab. They fed some of the caterpillars the same type of milkweed leaves that they would normally eat in the wild, and they fed the other caterpillars cabbage leaves, which don't contain cardenolides or any other poison at all. When all the caterpillars grew into adult butterflies, the butterflies either had cardenolides (from the milkweed leaves) or not (from the cabbage).

At this point, the Browers caught eight blue jays from the wild and kept them in a cage. They fed them the adult butterflies that had eaten cabbage. The blue jays acted completely normal. Then the scientists fed the butterflies that had eaten the milkweed leaves to the birds. *Wham!* All the blue jays gagged and threw up. The Browers wrote that the blue jays also showed a variety of behaviors that made it obvious they did not feel well: "excessive bill wiping, crouching, alternate fluffing and flattening of the feathers, erratic movements about the cage, jerky movements of the head, wings, and thoracic [chest] regions, partial closure of the eyes, eating of sand, twitching, and a generally sick appearance." Poor blue jays!

Thankfully, between twenty and sixty minutes after eating the milkweed-reared butterflies, the blue jays stopped barfing and returned to normal. Once they were feeling better, the Browers released the birds back to the wild.

The Browers repeated their experiment (oh, poor blue jays!). This time, they fed the monarch caterpillars different kinds of milkweed leaves. Some types of milkweed didn't make the blue jays as sick, or very sick at all, whereas others made the blue jays barf a lot. They also found that blue jays that barfed after eating monarch caterpillars or butterflies refused to eat any more monarch caterpillars or butterflies, even if those

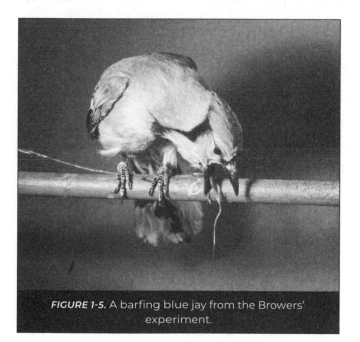

FIGURE 1-5. A barfing blue jay from the Browers' experiment.

caterpillars and butterflies had fed on leaves that were very low in cardenolides and would not have made the birds barf at all. The blue jays expected the monarchs to make them sick, and so they avoided them. This means that monarch caterpillars don't necessarily have to eat milkweed leaves that are rich in cardenolides in order to be protected from predators: The predators will avoid them anyway. The Browers called this **automimicry**. Automimicry is a good thing, because there are a number of different types of milkweed plants, and not having to choose only those types that are high in cardenolides increases the available area that female monarch butterflies can lay their eggs.

Once monarch caterpillars complete their metamorphosis and become butterflies, they no longer need to eat leaves. Their food is now in the form of nectar, the sugary liquid found in flowers. Using their long proboscis like a straw, monarch butterflies sip nectar from a variety of different flowers, not just milkweed. The nectar gives them the energy they need to fly and mate, which are the two main jobs of monarch butterflies. After a male monarch butterfly and a female monarch butterfly mate, the female lays her eggs on the underside of milkweed leaves, and the cycle begins again.

*FIGURE 1-6.* A female monarch butterfly (top) and a male monarch butterfly (bottom). Notice the two black splotches along the black veins on the male's hind wings, which females don't have. Females also have thicker black wing veins compared to males.

## CHAPTER TWO

# WHERE DO THEY GO?

Ever since he was a young boy, Dr. Fred Urquhart loved insects. Hours would slip by as he crouched down in a clover field near his home in Toronto, Canada, and watched with fascination the multitudes of buzzing, crawling, and flying creatures. He eventually started an insect collection and added monarch butterflies when he was about ten years old. When he was a teenager, he began to wonder where monarchs went in the winter. Where do they go to stay safe and warm? Or do they die off and somehow more butterflies are born in the spring?

This was 1927, long before the internet existed. Determined to find answers to his questions, young Dr. Urquhart met a local amateur butterfly collector who let him use his extensive library. He found an article that said monarchs wait out the winter season, or **over-winter**, under logs. So, Dr. Urquhart spent one winter trudging through the snow, lifting up any logs he could find. Although he found many types of butterflies, he found no monarchs.

He read articles published by scientists who studied monarchs, and he discovered that during late summer and early fall, thousands of monarch butterflies could be seen moving southward. Some scientists guessed that the monarchs were traveling to the coast of the Gulf of Mexico or to the Florida peninsula each winter, where it was much warmer compared to Canada and the northern United States. Perhaps these monarchs never returned, deciding to stay in more tropical weather. Maybe monarchs were seen each spring and summer in Canada and the northern United States because some of the butterflies and pupae overwintered under logs in breeding areas. But from his own winter searching, Dr. Urquhart was suspicious of these guesses. However, the fact that large clusters of monarchs are regularly seen moving south was interesting—and an important clue.

Then the young Dr. Urquhart came across an article written by a scientist in England named Dr. C. B. Williams. Dr. Williams suggested that butterflies migrate: They travel out of an area before winter arrives and return to the area in spring. Eventually, Dr. Williams published a large volume on all the data he had about the monarch butterfly, and he concluded that monarchs fly down to the Gulf Coast in Florida, stay for the winter, and then come back. However, there was no absolute proof of this; it was just a **theory**—a possible explanation that needed to be tested. At the time, it was considered quite impossible that monarchs might migrate in a way similar to many types of birds.

Time passed, and as an adult Dr. Urquhart ended up working at the Royal Ontario Museum in Toronto, Canada. He studied crickets and grasshoppers. He was quite talented, mostly thanks to his extensive musical training, which allowed him to hear and tell the difference between the many different types of chirps that crickets make. Despite his scientific progress studying these insects, the fact that no one knew for sure what happened to monarchs in winter still tickled the back of his mind.

Around 1935, Dr. Urquhart decided to start a side project to try to solve the mystery of the monarchs' overwintering journey and destination. Somehow, he needed to follow the monarchs wherever they flew. He knew that with birds, people attached a metal band to a bird's leg. Instructions printed on the band told where to send information about where the bird was found. Certainly, he couldn't attach a metal band to the leg of a butterfly. How could he mark an animal that was so much smaller and so much more delicate? The tricky task of how to tag monarchs began.

## HOW DO YOU TAG A BUTTERFLY?

For his first attempt at tagging monarchs, Dr. Urquhart used a small spray gun to apply various combinations of dyes and paint to the wings of the butterflies. He went out in the evenings and marked hundreds at a time as they clung in clusters to tree branches where they spent the night (these are often called **roosting sites**). He assumed that if someone found a butterfly with dye or paint on its wings, they would send it to the museum where he worked. But none of the butterflies were ever returned. Next, he tried using an ink stamp to apply numbers to the monarchs' wings, but that didn't work, either. He realized it wasn't enough to simply mark a butterfly. There had to be some sort of tag telling the person who found the butterfly what to do with it.

For his next attempt, Dr. Urquhart printed sheets of tags that read *Return to Museum, Toronto, Canada.* Each sheet had fifty tags that he cut out and glued to the monarchs' wings. He used a liquid glue, and what a mess it made! It spread everywhere: on other tags, all over his fingers, and he had to wait for the glue to dry before releasing the butterfly. Even worse, the tags and butterflies became tangled and sticky, and many of the butterflies couldn't stay airborne once the tag was glued onto them. He did manage to tag some butterflies, but none of these would be returned either.

**FIGURE 2-1.** Wintering roost of monarch butterflies on tree branches.

It was clear that the liquid glue method was not working. What about something similar to postage stamps? Dr. Urquhart asked the director of the Royal Ontario Museum if he could have some money to buy printed sheets of tags on postage stamp–type paper. Money was very tight, but the director reluctantly gave him ten dollars, which was a lot of money at the time. That was the first grant Dr. Urquhart received to study the monarch butterfly.

Dr. Urquhart purchased a sheet of these new tags and gave them a try. He just had to moisten the back of each tag and stick it to the upper surface of the monarch's right front wing. These new tags were mess-free and they stuck like a charm. But would the tags stay on if they became wet from rain? To test this, Dr. Urquhart set up a screened flight cage and put some tagged butterflies inside. He gently sprayed them with water and . . . all the tags fell off. However, he soon discovered that the tags stayed on much better if the scales on the butterfly's wing were removed. This was done by gently rubbing the wing between his thumb and forefinger, which didn't harm the butterfly at all. The tag was then folded over the edge of the butterfly's wing. He tagged as many butterflies as he could, and lo and behold, people returned hundreds of butterflies to him. Some of these butterflies were found up to 800 miles away!

By this time, World War II had begun. To help with the war efforts, Dr. Urquhart joined the Royal Canadian Air Force's meteorological department to assist with weather forecasting. His research with monarch butterflies was put on hold until the war ended in 1945. In 1945, he also met and married his wife, Norah, who was just as fascinated by monarchs as he was. Now they were a team of two who could continue the detective work of solving the mystery of the monarch butterfly migration.

Dr. Urquhart's tagging program started up again, using the postage stamp–type tags. Reports trickled in that these tags fell off under wet conditions. Dr. Urquhart and Norah[2] learned this themselves in 1954, when they were in California for a conference. They found some clusters of monarchs roosting in the branches of trees in Washington Park in the Monterey Peninsula. With the help of two students, they tagged over a thousand butterflies. It started to rain, and there was a light drizzle throughout the night, along

2. For clarity, I'll refer to her as Norah since she had the same last name as her husband.

with a heavy fog. When they visited the tagged area the next morning, the monarchs had not moved, but all the tags were scattered on the ground like soaked confetti.

It was time to find tags with some kind of waterproof glue.

Dr. Urquhart contacted a number of businesses as well as some friends of his who studied chemistry. He eventually discovered a label similar to those used for price tag stickers, which worked and passed the wet test. The flight of the butterflies was also not affected and tagging was much faster since the tags didn't have to be moistened. Dr. Urquhart and Norah could tag a butterfly in eight seconds, and if they came across an overnight roost in a tree, they were able to tag as many as 1,200 in a single morning.

Finally, the Urquharts had a way to track the monarchs to discover where they flew each year when summer shifts to fall. However, the next challenge was to find help to track them, since Dr. Urquhart and Norah couldn't be in many places at once along the monarchs' migratory route, wherever that may be. They also needed help tagging as many monarchs as possible. What could they do?

## HELPING HANDS FROM THE PUBLIC

To spread the word about their research, Norah wrote an article that was published in *Natural History* magazine, produced by the American Museum of Natural History. At the end of her article was a request for help with their research: If people found a tagged monarch, could they please let them know?

A few people responded. Then tagged monarchs began showing up in all kinds of towns and cities. Newspapers and magazines reported on the Urquharts' research, and that's when things really started to take off. Data flooded in from volunteers. People sent letters to the Urquharts to tell them the number on the tag of the monarch they happened to find. These people then released the butterfly to let it continue on its way. Or they would mail the actual tagged monarch to the Urquharts' lab, which was now at the University of Toronto. Often, people sent the monarchs alive, in a box lined with the flowers it was feeding on, and they included the date and place where it was captured. Norah handled all the communication with volunteers. She first wrote to the person who originally tagged the monarch to tell them that it was recaptured. She included the name and address of the person who had found the butterfly, along with the date and place where it was recaptured. Then she wrote to the person who found the tagged butterfly and told them where it was originally tagged, and she included a brief description of their research. With hundreds of people reporting their tagged monarch sightings, Norah did a lot of writing.

There was so much interest in the Urquharts' quest to find the monarch's migration route and overwintering site that they formed the Insect Migration Association (IMA). People joined from all over the world, and some members started sending donations. The National Geographic Society began sending them money, too. The Urquharts were quite grateful because they were now using 30,000 to 40,000 tags per year, which became very costly. To provide updates on their research, the Urquharts created an annual newsletter they named *Insect Migration Studies*. They mailed it out to individuals they referred to as their "research associates"—people who helped tag and recover monarchs, reported monarch sightings, and otherwise helped the Urquharts with their research.

When the Urquharts received a tagged monarch, or when someone wrote to them about a tagged monarch, they put two pins in a map of North America that hung on a wall. One pin was placed where the monarch was originally tagged. The other pin was placed where the tagged monarch was seen or recaptured. Then they joined the two pins with a black thread. This line of the butterfly's flight was called a **release-recapture line (RRL)**. Over time, a pattern emerged on the map: The monarchs' flight paths began in northeast Canada and the United States, then continued southwest across the midwestern United States, and ended at various points along the US Gulf Coast and in Texas.

The Urquharts hit the road. They drove in their car and they took flights. In total they covered almost 20,000 miles, searching for mobs of gathering monarchs in Texas and along the Gulf Coast. But alas, they found none. Then the Urquharts recalled that a number of tagged monarchs had been recaptured in Mexico. Perhaps the butterflies passed through Texas on their way to a destination in Mexico? The Urquharts left Texas, crossed the border into Mexico, and resumed their search. Again, they found nothing.

Tired and frustrated, the Urquharts decided to reach out to the public again for help. In late 1972, Norah wrote to newspapers in Mexico about their project, asking for volunteers to report sightings of large clusters of monarchs and help with tagging. In February 1973, she received a letter from Mexico City written by a white American named Kenneth Brugger. He and his partner, a Mexican woman named Catalina Trail,[3] enjoyed roaming the Mexican countryside and were very enthusiastic about helping. The Urquharts sent Brugger and Trail pictures of what monarch butterflies look like and clues to where their overwintering sites might be, based on information from tagging efforts.

Then, on the evening of January 2, 1975, the Urquharts' phone rang. It was Brugger.[4] He was breathless with excitement. "We have located the colony!" he exclaimed. "We have found them—millions of monarchs—in evergreen trees beside a mountain clearing!" Brugger explained that he and Trail met some Mexican woodcutters who said they saw swarming butterflies, and they had pointed the way.

The Urquharts announced in their annual newsletter that the overwintering site had been found. They did not reveal the exact location, but they wrote that they hoped to provide more details in next year's

---

3. Catalina Trail's birth name was Catalina Aguado. She changed her last name to Trail after getting married in 1995.

4. In Dr. Urquhart's 1976 article in *National Geographic*, he states that Brugger called him on January 9, 1975. However, two other sources, including an interview with Catalina Trail, state that he called him on January 2.

newsletter. Dr. Urquhart had a heart condition and could not travel right away, but he and Norah flew to Mexico the following year, in 1976. Brugger, Trail, and *National Geographic* photographer Bianca Lavies went with them to Sierra Chincua, about five miles north of the town of Angangueo in the State of Michoacán, where they recruited some local guides. Once they reached a high summit, they left their vehicle and set out on foot. Although they were surrounded by a forest filled with majestic pine, fir, and other evergreen trees, the hike was treacherous. With the steep climb and the strain on his body from the high altitude, Dr. Urquhart wondered if he would make it alive.

They finally arrived at a clearing—and saw them. Dr. Urquhart described his experience in the well-known article he wrote for *National Geographic.*

> I gazed in amazement at the sight. Butterflies—millions upon millions of monarch butterflies! They clung in tightly packed masses to every branch and trunk of the tall, gray-green oyamel trees, which is a type of fir tree. They swirled through the air like autumn leaves and carpeted the

ground in their flaming myriads on this Mexican mountainside. Breathless from the altitude, my legs trembling from the climb, I muttered aloud, "Unbelievable! What a glorious, incredible sight!"

Sunlight streamed through the branches, and, as it warmed the air, some of the butterflies fluttered down to the ground to drink water from puddles. These monarchs were quite sluggish and clung to anything, including the hats, coats, and faces of the Urquharts, Brugger, Trail, and their guides.

One of the guides, Juan Sanchez, added up all the tall oyamel trees. He estimated that there were 1,000 trees in total, each one completely covered in monarchs. That's a lot of butterflies!

The great mystery that Dr. Urquhart had been chasing for years was finally solved. He wrote in his *National Geographic* article that as everyone marveled at the breathtaking scene before them, there was a loud *CRACK!* A branch about three inches thick broke under the weight of all the monarchs perched upon it. It crashed to the ground, spilling butterflies everywhere. Dr. Urquhart stooped to examine the mass of fallen, fluttering monarchs. There, upon a wing of one of the monarchs, was a white tag! Dr. Urquhart's hand shook as he carefully picked up the butterfly and placed it in his palm. It was definitely one of their tags. Later, Dr. Urquhart wrote, "I could not have been more excited if I had uncovered a buried treasure of fabulous value." Dr. Urquhart was enormously lucky to have found one of their tagged monarchs. "Here I had undeniable proof," Dr. Urquhart later wrote, "that monarch butterflies overwintering on this mountain had come from distant breeding grounds."[5]

Everyone was anxious to learn where the tagged monarch had come from. When they returned to their motel, they asked Mitzi, the motel owner, to place a phone call from their remote Mexican village to the University of Toronto. After what felt like an eternity, they finally reached the Urquharts' assistant. They told the assistant that the tag on the monarch read *PS 397*. She checked their files and reported that the butterfly had been tagged on September 5, 1975, four months earlier, by a teacher named Jim Gilbert and two students

---

5. Urquhart described his own discovery of a tagged monarch at Sierra Chincua in the August 1976 issue of *National Geographic* magazine. However, as we'll see in the next chapter, Trail and Brugger discovered two tagged butterflies a year earlier when they found the overwintering sites.

from his class in Chaska, Minnesota. The butterfly had flown 1,225 miles from where it was originally tagged.

Before the Urquharts left the overwintering site, more than 10,000 butterflies were tagged with bright pink tags. If any of those butterflies were found later, the Urquharts would immediately know that they came from Sierra Chincua. Sure enough, two monarchs with bright pink tags were found the following April in northern Texas, 1,000 miles from where they had spent the winter in Mexico.

In the course of their research, the Urquharts received the help of over 3,000 people. These citizens helped tag butterflies, catch tagged butterflies, and report where they had been found. Dr. Urquhart collected about 3,800 newspaper and magazine articles featuring the work that he and Norah had done. They never dreamed that their quest to find the monarch overwintering site would become so involved. In 1998, Dr. Fred and Norah Urquhart were awarded the Order of Canada, the highest award given to Canadian citizens to recognize their contributions to the country.

Dr. Fred Urquhart passed away on November 2, 2002, at the age of ninety. Norah Urquhart passed away on March 13, 2009, also at the age of ninety. As we will see later in this book, although their own journey of discovery with monarch butterflies came to a close, many other researchers picked up where they left off.

Dr. Fred and Norah Urquhart's efforts, perseverance, and detective work lasted decades. They never gave up seeking the answers to their questions. They certainly deserved recognition for their part in uncovering the monarch overwintering sites for the larger world. However, they did not do it alone, and as we'll see, theirs is not the complete tale.

## CHAPTER THREE

# MORE TO THE STORY

In its August 1976 issue, *National Geographic* magazine published a spectacular article written by Dr. Urquhart titled "Found at Last: The Monarch's Winter Home." The piece included photographs of millions of monarch butterflies filling the sky. The cover featured Catalina Trail sitting at an overwintering site, arms outstretched, with monarchs clinging to her head, arms, and legs. Monarch butterflies completely carpet the trees and ground around her. Never before had people seen or heard of such mass congregations of monarch butterflies. Or had they? Dr. Urquhart's famous *National Geographic* article is only one side of the story behind the discovery of the monarch overwintering grounds. What follows are two other perspectives: that of citizen scientist Catalina Trail and of the Mexican people who share land with the overwintering monarchs.

## CATALINA TRAIL

In the 1950s in Michoacán, Mexico, a little girl lay on her stomach in the dirt watching butterflies. She saw mourning cloaks with their deep chocolate-brown wings edged with a buttery yellow. Where the yellow and brown met, there were flecks of sky blue, as though someone used a fine paintbrush to dab blue paint along the length of the wings. Tiger swallowtails fluttered by, cream-colored with black stripes. They also had flecked, dotted lines along their wings, as though the painter couldn't help but continue their art. And then there were the monarchs, brilliant and striking in orange and black. The girl watched as they landed so softly on the flowers. They extended their long, curled-up tongue, sipped, lifted, landed, and sipped again.

The girl was Catalina Trail, and she dreamed of traveling the world and going to college. "I was a crazy, buggy girl," said Trail later in life when she was living in Austin, Texas. She remembered spending many days watching butterflies and other insects.

When Trail was twenty-two years old, she met

a man named Kenneth Brugger. He was an inventor and textile consultant from the United States. Together they decided to travel across Mexico in a Winnebago, fulfilling a dream of hers. Trail still had a passion for butterflies, so she made nets so they could chase them during their travels. Along the way she taught Brugger about butterflies, too. "He didn't know one butterfly from another," Trail recalled. She would soon fix that. Day after day they traveled, seeing sights across beautiful Mexico. Trail couldn't have been happier. Little did she know her amazing adventure was about to begin.

## HELP WANTED

One day in February 1973, when Trail was twenty-three, she and Brugger spied a notice in a Mexico City newspaper. It was written by Norah Urquhart, a woman up in Canada, asking for volunteers to search for and tag monarch butterflies. Traveling and chasing butterflies, this time with a purpose instead of simply for pleasure—it was as though the notice was written especially for Trail. But she felt a nagging tug in her gut. She wanted to attend college at some point. Helping Norah and her husband, Fred, would leave no time for classes.

What should she do? In the end, she decided to put college on hold and help the Urquharts. The opportunity was too irresistible. Trail also realized she had advantages that the Urquharts did not: She spoke Spanish and had knowledge of Mexican culture and the countryside. This would be extremely useful as they explored the more remote areas of the country. "Ken answered the ad," recalled Trail. "I was the little Mexican girl; he called me Cathy. He was the big American guy. I was rusty on speaking English, but I could read and write it. So he communicated, and I typed." Trail would later prove to be invaluable in the search for the overwintering sites.

The Urquharts were thrilled that the team of two were willing to search for monarchs. Trail and Brugger packed up their Winnebago and headed for the mountains near Zitácuaro, about a hundred miles west of Mexico City. Trail was buzzing with excitement.

After about a year of driving around and chasing monarchs, Trail and Brugger traveled to Toronto, Canada, to visit the Urquharts in person. "They told us more about their research and how the monarchs disappeared into a 'black hole' after they left Texas," Trail said. The Urquharts did not know where the monarchs spent the winter. Trail was also curious about where the monarchs went. The Urquharts thought they might overwinter somewhere in Mexico. Trail and Brugger decided to help the Urquharts solve the mystery of the location of the monarch overwintering site. They loaded up their Winnebago once again and headed back to Zitácuaro, where they had seen great numbers of monarchs. This time, they brought along a Honda motorcycle and a basenji dog named Kola.

Once Trail and Brugger were back in the Trans-Mexican Volcanic Belt, known locally as the Sierra Nevada, they set out each day at 4:30 in the morning. Brugger drove the motorcycle, Trail used binoculars to search the mountains, and Kola sat between them. After driving for a while, they would hide the motorcycle and continue on foot. Most days they hiked about eleven miles, and they didn't return until sundown. They slept in the Winnebago, but sometimes they spent the night in a motel if they wanted electricity and a hot shower. They always set out early in the morning so they could get to their location without being seen. Occasionally, they would encounter local people who lived in the mountains. These people were very curious about what Trail and Brugger were doing, since the mountains were not a popular tourist destination. Trail told them they were looking for monarch butterflies. "They were OK with that," she remembered.

How did Trail and Brugger know where to go each day? They saw monarchs near the mountains, and they knew the butterflies needed a certain temperature and humidity. They bought topographical maps in Mexico City and focused on certain areas. "I always wrote down where we went, temperatures, altitudes, wind direction, and how many monarchs we saw," Trail recalled. "I kept a total of around forty legal pads and composition books, filled with data."

January 2, 1975, started like any other day. Trail, Brugger, and Kola were now on the Cerro Pelón mountain. They set off at 4:00 a.m. on their motorcycle with their walking sticks and three backpacks, which held all their equipment: cameras, film, maps, water, food, and Trail's notebooks. The weather was miserable. Trail wrote in her notebook that morning that snow and rain had fallen, the sky was covered in gray clouds, and the temperature was hovering around the freezing point. As they trekked up the mountainside, it became so steep that they hired a local man with a horse to help them carry their packs. As they hiked along, Trail felt the ground become squishy and soft. Soon, with each footstep, her legs sunk into the mulch up to her thighs. Even Kola was struggling. The man with the horse was afraid of coral snakes in those parts. The snakes' flashy red, black, yellow, or white stripes are a signal that their bite is highly poisonous. "I told my feet that there were no coral snakes and kept going," said Trail.

As they trudged up the mountain, Trail and Brugger fanned out a bit. They thought that walking along slightly different paths increased their chances of finding butterflies. It was now late in the afternoon and Trail was tired and hungry. But she kept going. She was quite a bit ahead of Brugger, Kola, and the man with the horse. She alternated between looking down to watch where she stepped and looking up to scan her surroundings. Exhausted, she watched her feet for a bit longer, feeling a trickle of sweat creep down her back. When she eventually looked up, she was slammed by what she saw.

"I need the camera! I see them! I see them! Up here!" Trail yelled.

She heard Brugger's footsteps as he ran up to her. She sensed him standing next to her, but she couldn't look away from what she saw.

Monarch butterflies. Millions upon millions of monarch butterflies. They covered the branches, the tree trunks, and the ground. They were everywhere.

"Oh my God," said Brugger.

Trail and Brugger stood in silence. They couldn't believe it. "I will never get over seeing so many butterflies at one time," said Trail. "I don't have the words to describe what I saw."

Trail and Brugger walked for a while, being careful where they stepped so they didn't kill any of the monarchs. "Wow, wow," they kept whispering. They didn't want to disturb the butterflies in this incredible sanctuary. Eventually, they came to a clearing. "Hey," called the man with the horse, who was quite far behind them. "It's really getting late!" There was no way Trail was leaving now. Thinking the man was probably hungry, and to persuade him to stay longer, she called back, "I have chocolates in my bag." He ended up eating all of them.

Overwhelmed, Trail squatted down. She gently nudged away the monarchs and lay on the ground on her back. She crossed her arms over her chest. It wasn't long before monarchs covered her body from head to toe. She could even feel their scratchy feet on her face. Filled with awe and amazement, she wished everyone could see what she was seeing and feel what she was feeling.

Sunlight began to fade as Trail and Brugger continued to marvel at the monarchs. They had to make their way back down the mountain before dark. Trail felt a swell of dread. "My heart was crying and my spirit was low," she recalled. She asked Brugger what they should do now. "We call Fred," he said.

"Then what?" asked Trail. "Now there will be hordes of people here and they'll destroy everything."

"That's why we don't tell anyone."

And they didn't tell anyone, except the Urquharts. Brugger managed to reach them by telephone that evening. The Urquharts were ecstatic. Finally, after years and years of research, a monarch overwintering site was found! But they agreed with Trail and Brugger that they should keep the location of the monarchs secret.

Thirty miles from where Trail and Brugger first found a colony of monarchs, they encountered another overwintering site: Sierra Chincua. It was here that they made a spectacular discovery: two white-colored tags used by the Urquharts and the Insect Migration Association. One tag had the serial number S2-294. This butterfly had been tagged by Mrs. C. Emery of

Nevada, Missouri. The other butterfly had a homemade tag displaying the number 84 and had been tagged by John McClusky of Fredericksburg, Texas.[6] Trail marveled at how monarch butterflies came from across North America to gather for the winter, only about 120 miles from where she was born. She continued the search with Brugger, and over the next few days, they found four more monarch colonies.

**COVER STORY**

A year later, in 1976, Dr. Urquhart and Norah were able to travel to Mexico. Trail and Brugger brought them to Sierra Chincua, the second monarch overwintering site they had found. Along with them was *National Geographic* photographer Bianca Lavies. Despite the agreement between Trail, Brugger, and the Urquharts to keep the overwintering sites a secret, Dr. Urquhart wrote an article about this trip and the discovery of the monarch overwintering sites. It was published in the August 1976 issue of *National Geographic* magazine.

---

6. In their 1975 *Insect Migration Studies* newsletter, the Urquharts list these two recovered tags in their regular section titled "Recapture Records for Monarch Butterflies." However, it is not clear in the newsletter that these tags were found by Trail and Brugger and that they came from an overwintering site. Also, Dr. Urquhart does not mention Trail and Brugger's recovery of these tags in his 1976 *National Geographic* article.

The article is fourteen pages long. It mostly tells the story of the research Dr. Urquhart did with Norah and finally seeing the masses of monarchs overwintering in Mexico. Despite Trail's role in finding the overwintering site and being featured on the *National Geographic* cover, in the whole article, she is mentioned only twice. The first time is in a photo caption at the beginning of the article, where it simply states, "Cathy Brugger and her husband, Kenneth, discovered the site where millions rendezvous." The second time is halfway through the article, where Dr. Urquhart simply wrote, "Ken Brugger doubled his field capability by marrying a bright and delightful Mexican, Cathy." Trail was shocked and deeply saddened when she read the article. Her years of hard work, trekking up and down mountains every day, calculating where the monarchs could be hiding, taking meticulous notes, and putting college on hold, was all overshadowed by other people's biases about her gender and race. She also thought the Urquharts would keep her discovery a secret to protect the monarchs, yet here they were, publicly announcing it in a popular magazine. "I was disappointed and disagreed with what happened after we discovered the butterflies," Trail said.

Although the world learned of the monarch over-wintering sites after the *National Geographic* article was published, Dr. Urquhart did not reveal the exact locations of the monarch colonies. Controversy followed. At the heart of it was the crucial question: What do you do when you find such an incredible natural phenomenon, like the monarch overwintering site, that much of the world doesn't know about? Do you not tell anyone else? Or do you share it with the world? Should these sites be open to the public? Dr. Urquhart had said he wanted to keep it a secret, yet by publishing his story in *National Geographic*, he obviously wanted international attention. Other researchers thought they should be told the secret so they, too, could learn more about monarch biology and survival. Trail was saddened to witness this drama and wanted no part of it. She decided to remain silent.

As the years went by, Trail's life took a turn away from the monarchs. She and Brugger eventually divorced, and he passed away in 1998 at the age of eighty. She married a rehabilitation counselor named George Trail, and soon after, she earned a social work degree from the University of Texas at Austin. She went on to work as a case manager and counselor, helping people who struggle with psychiatric and substance use disorders.

She retired and spends much of her time gardening and looking up at the stars. Her appreciation and admiration for the monarchs, and nature in general, did not fade. "I searched for the monarchs because of the love I have for all insects and all of nature," she reflected. "For the awe that they provoke in me in all the beautiful and ugly ways. I care about the truth and the marvelous way that nature works in all of us."

In 2011, a film crew decided to make a documentary called *Flight of the Butterflies* about monarch butterflies and the work of Dr. Fred and Norah Urquhart. They hired a detective to find Trail, and they asked her to be a historical adviser during their filming, which she agreed to. In 2016, Trail was interviewed by Sheryl Smith-Rodgers for a three-page article titled "Maiden of the Monarchs" in *Texas Parks & Wildlife* magazine, which tells her story about chasing monarch butterflies.

These are the only two instances when Trail decided to tell her story. While her silence on the monarchs is understandable and her privacy deserves to be respected, it is important that a book about monarch butterflies include her story, because she has been largely excluded from the history of the scientific discoveries about monarch overwintering. Without her, who knows if we would have discovered where the monarchs spend their winters?

## THE MONARCHS' MEXICAN NEIGHBORS

While searching the Mexican mountains for the monarch overwintering grounds, Trail and Brugger encountered Indigenous communities and people who live in **ejidos**: communal land where people live and farm. These local communities took care of the forests, which included felling trees sustainably. They had rights to live on the land and cut and extract wood, and they used and sold the wood for fuel, heat, and making wooden tools and goods.[7] The monarch overwintering grounds were therefore not an unpeopled wilderness; the butterflies shared land with human neighbors. Did these people see or know about large overwintering clusters of monarchs before they were discovered by Trail? Oral histories shared in 2020 with Patricio Moreno Rojas, Dr. Ellen Sharp, and Dr. Will Wright suggest that they did. These histories presented yet

7. In 1930, after the Mexican Revolution, land in Mexico was redistributed to various groups of people. If Indigenous communities could prove to the Mexican government that their land had been illegally taken from them by colonizers, they could apply to have it restored to them. This process is known as restitution.

another side to the story of the monarch butterflies and are important in our understanding of them.

## COWS AND CANALS

Elidió Moreno de Jesús lives in Macheros, a village in the State of México. He is a retired forester who worked in Cerro Pelón for a state conservation agency called Comisión Estatal de Parques Naturales y de la Fauna (CEPANAF, State Commission of Natural Parks and Wildlife). He recalled seeing overwintering monarchs when he was a boy living in Ejido El Capulín in the 1940s. "When we were herding cattle, we would go into the forest to look for the cows that wandered off so we could get the herd back together . . . and there in the forest the branches were loaded with [butterflies]." He didn't know where they came from or where they went.

Elidió's cousin Leonel Moreno Espinoza also lives in Macheros and grew up in Ejido El Capulín.[8] Like Elidió, Leonel is a retired forester with CEPANAF who worked in Cerro Pelón. He remembered elders talking

---

8. In Latin America, people usually have two surnames. The first comes from the paternal side of the family (Moreno) and the second comes from the spouse's side (de Jesús). That's why Leonel and Elidió share the name Moreno (as cousins), but their final names (de Jesús and Espinoza) are different since they married different people. For clarity, I will refer to them by their first names.

about where the monarchs came from. "Some older folks said that butterflies were born from the oyamel seeds, others said that there was a cave in Cerro Pelón and that butterflies came from there." Leonel said he never saw the overwintering colonies as a child, but he knew about them. He did see many monarchs drinking from a spring that landholders converted into a canal. "The canal was filled with water, then the butterflies went down into the water and we played with them . . . but we did not know where they came from or where they were going, how they were born or anything. We just saw them there in the water, we walked around a lot of butterflies, but in all that time as a child seeing butterflies, I never went to the colony, never."

At one point in Leonel's interview, Dr. Sharp mentioned Trail and Brugger. "There is a well-known history in the rest of the world," she told him, "about a couple, a Mexican and her gringo boyfriend, that they discovered the colony here in Cerro Pelón, next to Carditos, but below and that was on January 5, 1975."[9]

"Possibly yes," replied Leonel. "I no longer remember . . ."

---

9. As we saw earlier, there is some disagreement about the exact date when Trail found the Cerro Pelón overwintering site.

## DISCOVERY OF THE CERRO PELÓN COLONY

The interviews revealed that at some point—the date is not clear—two Canadians contacted the governor of the State of México, Jorge Jiménez Cantú. They said they were looking for monarch overwintering sites. Dr. Sharp and Dr. Wright suspected that these two Canadians were Norah and Dr. Urquhart, but they do not have definitive evidence to support this educated guess. A man named Jesús Ávila Montes de Oca—or Don Jesús, as Leonel and his friends called him—knew the governor and often went deer hunting in Cerro Pelón. "Hey, Bear," the governor said to Jesús (the governor's nickname for him was Bear), "you know where the butterflies are?" Jesús said he would find out. He summoned his hunting guides: Elidió, Leonel, and Valentín Velázquez. Jesús was from a family of powerful estate owners called hacendados, and he was used to giving orders. "Don Jesús knew that the butterfly arrived here, but he did not know where exactly it was," said Leonel. "Don Jesús came to us and said, 'Go look for the butterflies, it's urgent.'"

The men began their search. Leonel and Valentín managed to find a "cloud of butterflies" flying from one side of a meadow to another, so they followed them into the forest. It began to rain quite hard, so the two men found shelter and waited. When the rain stopped, the butterflies were nowhere to be seen. Leonel and Valentín went home. The next day, Elidió and Valentín went back, "and they found [the colony] right there where we'd been stopped by the rain," said Leonel. Dr. Sharp noticed that Leonel sounded a bit frustrated as he recalled missing out on discovering the colony by a day. When Leonel finally did see the colony, "they were fluttering around the trees, I felt that my heart was pounding in my chest to see so many butterflies, as the trees were covered."

Valentín's son, Emilio Velázquez Moreno, is a forest guardian for Butterflies & Their People, a nonprofit organization Dr. Sharp co-founded that employs local people to protect the Cerro Pelón Monarch Butterfly Sanctuary. Emilio told Dr. Sharp, "My dad was one of the first to find the butterflies here [in Cerro Pelón]. In fact, he was the one who found them." He said his father brought butterflies down to Jesús in bags. "He made some holes for them [in the bags] and he came down [the mountain] . . . he brought down several bags, for Don Jesús Ávila, to prove that they had been found." Dr. Sharp said that some people credit Valentín with the discovery of the Cerro Pelón overwintering colony, whereas others emphasize the role of Jesús.

A Mexican broadcasting station named Televisa interviewed Jesús and the Urquharts about the discovery. After the documentary aired, Televisa's president was flooded with letters from people across Mexico. Jesús worried that people would be rushing to the forest to see the butterflies. How would this tide of tourists affect the overwintering sites? Jesús used his political connections to secure work for all three men—Elidió, Leonel, and Valentín—as **guardabosques**, or forest rangers, for CEPANAF. The three men became some of the few community members in their ejido to enjoy secure employment. They patrolled the forest, aiming to prevent logging wherever butterflies roosted. They did not have the authority to fine or arrest people for cutting down trees, but they could talk to them and file reports with their superiors. The men also maintained trails, built firebreaks, and regulated tourist access.

**MANY VOICES**
Reflecting on what he learned from the interviews and from his additional research, Dr. Wright thought that the locals at Cerro Pelón would say that the Urquharts did not "discover" the monarchs' overwintering grounds. Locals knew that monarch butterflies came and went

each year, and that some kind of roosting sites existed. Rather, what Trail, Brugger, and the Urquharts' efforts confirmed was a tri-national migration of butterflies. "In any important scientific quest there are always multiple people working on it," said Dr. Wright. "We give credit to one person, but there's never just one person working on something that's important."

When it comes to the monarch butterfly migration, why hasn't the wider world known about the role of Trail and the Indigenous and local people of Cerro Pelón? Dr. Urquhart's *National Geographic* article was based on his perspective and on his version of events. It was from his position as a scientist and "northerner." Dr. Wright made the important point that Norah and Dr. Urquhart didn't speak Spanish. This would have significantly affected their search in Mexico for the monarch overwintering grounds and the people with whom they interacted. "Another layer is in some ways Catalina was an outsider, too," Dr. Wright said. "I mean, she grows up in Morelia and she speaks Spanish and is familiar with Michoacán, but still she's more middle class . . . Most people that live in the ejidos and Indigenous communities are very poor, so there's a class barrier. Plus, she has this white husband." Although Trail could speak their language, Indigenous and ejido communities were suspicious of her intentions, considering how colonizers have treated Indigenous people throughout history. If they gave Trail information, what would happen to their land rights that they had to fight for in the past? Would their communal forest turn into a butterfly habitat? Dr. Wright recalled something Ana Moreno, niece of Leonel and Elidió, said to him. She lives in Cerro Pelón, and she told him "that silence is a form of conservation. Keeping a secret conserves the land in a sense."

As we will see, many consequences followed from Dr. Urquhart's decision to publish the "discovery" of the overwintering grounds in *National Geographic*. There were consequences for the butterflies, for their human neighbors, and for science. Next, we will explore how the "discovery" fueled the determination of scientists to learn more about monarch butterflies.

# CHAPTER FOUR

# SQUABBLING SCIENTISTS

The August 1976 issue of *National Geographic* magazine caused quite a splash with both the public and the scientific community. Outside the local people, most others had no idea that such an incredible natural spectacle existed. It was like a miracle revealed to the rest of the world.

There was one scientist in particular who was struck by the "discovery" Dr. Urquhart revealed in *National Geographic*. Remember the barfing blue jay experiments by Drs. Jane and Lincoln Brower in Chapter One? Dr. Lincoln Brower wasn't interested just in whether monarchs make blue jays sick. He also wanted to know where monarchs go in winter. While the Urquharts were busy testing sticky tags on monarch butterflies' wings, Dr.

Brower was devising his own monarch tracking method. He reached out to Dr. Urquhart in an attempt to share their scientific insights. Unfortunately, what began as a friendly correspondence unraveled into a bitter rivalry.

## POISONOUS FINGERPRINTS

Dr. Brower heard about the Urquharts' tagging efforts and their quest to find the monarch overwintering grounds. He sent them a copy of one of his published research articles about poisonous cardenolides in milkweed, along with a letter asking if they knew of any monarch clustering sites in Mexico. Dr. Urquhart wrote back, "If we do find the areas of concentration, we will certainly be able to arrange for specimens to be sent to you, or, if you wish, give you exact locations and names of the persons to contact." While Dr. Brower waited to hear from Dr. Urquhart, he busied himself with his own research.

Dr. Brower began to design how monarch butterflies could be tracked. His thinking was this: Milkweed species across North America differ in cardenolide content. If he caught a monarch butterfly and figured out what kind of milkweed the monarch fed on as a caterpillar, he could narrow down the region from which the butterfly came.

With assistance from some chemist colleagues, Dr. Brower discovered that monarch butterflies each have a cardenolide "fingerprint." This fingerprint depends on which type of milkweed the butterfly fed on as a caterpillar. To see a butterfly's cardenolide fingerprint, the butterfly has to be frozen, dried out, and ground up into a powder. The powder is mixed with some liquids and passed through a few machines. Eventually, the mixture is spread onto a glass plate, and it looks like what is shown in Figure 4-1. This figure shows fingerprints from twelve different monarch butterflies. Three of the butterflies had fed on poke milkweed (*Asclepias exaltata*) in Virginia as caterpillars, three had fed on sandhill or pinewoods milkweed (*Asclepias humistrata*) in Florida, three had fed on common milkweed (*Asclepias syriaca*) in North Dakota and Minnesota, and three had fed on green milkweed (*Asclepias viridis*) in Florida. If you look at the blotches and smudges, you'll see that the pattern for each butterfly that ate the same type of milkweed is very similar, but the patterns differ quite a bit between different types of milkweed. These are the cardenolide "fingerprints."

Dr. Brower saw much potential for this technique. If a monarch butterfly was captured, its "fingerprint" would show what species of milkweed it fed upon as a caterpillar, and the butterfly's origins could be traced. He felt that the jackpot would come once we knew where monarchs go in the wintertime, because samples of butterflies could be taken from the overwintering grounds, they could be "fingerprinted," and then we

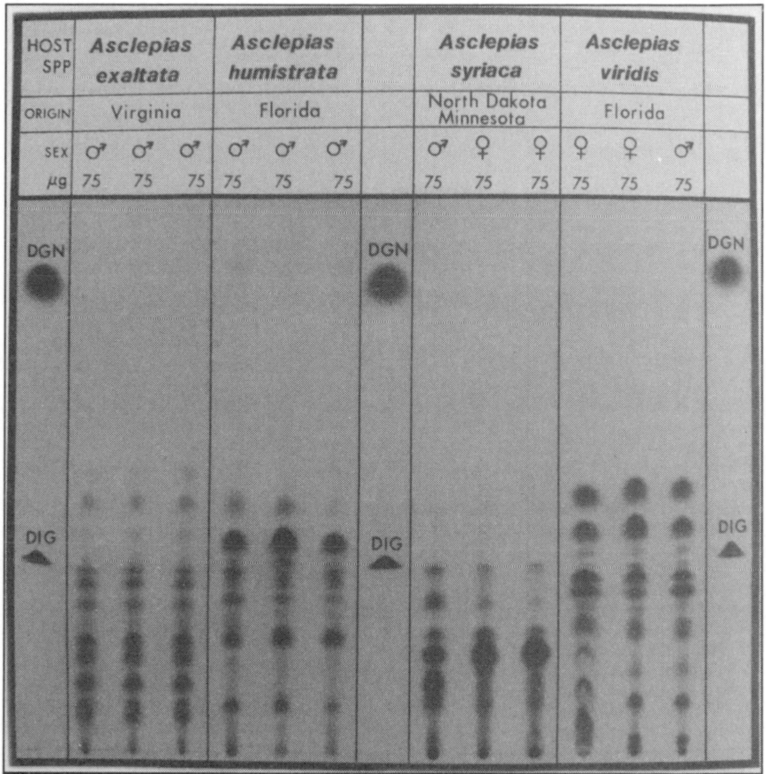
HOST SPP
Asclepias exaltata
Asclepias humistrata
Asclepias syriaca
Asclepias viridis
ORIGIN
Virginia
Florida
North Dakota Minnesota
Florida
SEX
♂ ♂ ♂ ♂ ♂ ♂ ♂ ♀ ♀ ♀ ♀ ♂
µg
75 75 75 75 75 75 75 75 75 75 75 75
DGN
DGN
DGN
DIG
DIG
DIG

***FIGURE 4-1.*** Cardenolide "fingerprints" for twelve butterflies that fed on four different types of milkweed as caterpillars.

could figure out where they originally came from. It would be a whole new form of tagging, different from the physical tags the Urquharts were using. All he needed was the location in Mexico where monarch butterflies migrate to. But would the Urquharts help him?

**SECRETS, SQUABBLING, AND SEARCHING**

While Dr. Lincoln Brower and his colleagues were perfecting the technique of "fingerprinting" monarch butterflies, Trail and Brugger were close to discovering the monarch overwintering grounds in Mexico. In late 1974, Dr. Urquhart mailed Dr. Brower some milkweed seeds from Mexico that were apparently collected by Trail and Brugger during their travels. Unaware of Trail's discovery of the monarch overwintering site on January 2, 1975, Dr. Brower wrote to Dr. Urquhart to thank him for the seeds. In his letter he asked, "Have you found where the monarch butterfly overwinters in Mexico yet? It must be a spectacular sight to see." Dr. Brower waited eagerly for a response.

But a response never came. Dr. Brower learned about Trail's huge discovery from the Urquharts' annual newsletter. He was hurt that he didn't hear about it from Dr. Urquhart himself, given their friendly correspondence up to that point. Dr. Brower called Dr. Urquhart and asked him to share the location of the newly found monarch overwintering site. Dr. Urquhart said he couldn't reveal it before his article in *National Geographic* was published; however, after the article was in print, he could tell him.

At this point, Dr. Brower was quite frustrated, but he wasn't going to give up. He telephoned the National Geographic Society directly and asked whether they would share the location of the site. The society responded that they "had adopted a policy not to divulge the location of the colonies prior to the publication of the discovery in their journal." Dr. Brower tried to emphasize that he was a scientist whose intentions were nothing but good. Unfortunately, the National Geographic Society would not budge.

Finally, the famous August 1976 issue of *National Geographic* was released. Then the Urquharts published an article in the September 1976 issue of the *Journal of the Lepidopterists' Society*. In both articles, Dr. Urquhart gave only a vague description of where the overwintering sites were. Despite his previous promises, he still had not told Dr. Brower the location. Dr. Brower tried yet again. He wrote Dr. Urquhart a letter in which he hid his mounting frustration and instead took the high road. He congratulated him on the discovery in Mexico. He invited him to Amherst College, where Dr. Brower was a professor, to give a lecture on his discovery. And finally, he gently reminded Dr. Urquhart of their past conversation in which Dr. Urquhart agreed to share the location of the overwintering site. He stated that he would like to go to the site in Mexico so he could collect samples and continue his research. His intention for visiting the site was to further science—nothing more.

Dr. Urquhart eventually wrote back, months later, with his most distressing letter yet. He said that he had met with the National Geographic Society, including editorial staff and the president of the society, and they had "agreed that the site should not be divulged since it was anticipated that many people, collectors, film makers, etc. would wish to visit and, as happened in other similar situations, destroy it." Dr. Brower was furious. But his anger fueled his determination. He would find the Mexican overwintering sites himself.

Before beginning his search, Dr. Brower scrutinized the articles that the Urquharts published for any clues about the sites in Mexico. In the article in the *Journal of the Lepidopterists' Society*, Dr. Brower found three clues and a puzzle. The three clues were (italics added): "The overwintering colony . . . was located *on the slope of a volcanic mountain* situated in the *northern part of the State of Michoacán*, Mexico, at a height of *slightly over 3000 m.*" Dr. Brower could use these clues to piece together the overwintering location. And the puzzle? The "ground was covered with monarch wings that we saw falling from the trees." Dr. Brower knew that falling monarch wings meant one thing: Birds were eating the butterflies. But why were birds eating the monarchs? The butterflies were supposed to be poisonous with cardenolides! Now Dr. Brower was even more excited to find the overwintering site.

With his colleague Dr. William (Bill) Calvert, and with the help of a librarian, Dr. Brower obtained a topographic map of Mexico that showed the elevations of the mountains. They placed a clear plastic sheet over the map and circled all areas that satisfied the three clues: the slope of a volcanic mountain, the northern part of the State of Michoacán, and an altitude of slightly over 9,842 feet. Dr. Calvert and Dr. Brower managed to narrow down where to look. On December 26, 1976, Dr. Calvert set off for Mexico with a small group of friends. On New Year's Eve, Dr. Brower's phone rang at his home in Amherst, Massachusetts. It was Dr. Calvert. He said that after a "long, complicated, tedious, and frustrating piece of detective work involving a number of people," they had located Sierra Chincua—one of the sites that Trail and Brugger had found previously. They had found it with the help of the nephew of Municipal President Manuel Arriaga Nava, from the town of Angangueo, who acted as their guide.

Dr. Calvert and his team returned to the United States, and he and Dr. Brower set off on a second expedition to the site on January 22, 1977. After seeing the monarch colony for the first time, Dr. Brower wrote:

> At first, we could not find the butterflies because the day was overcast, and they were inactive. But as we walked farther down a slope, I noticed changes in the patterns of light through the trees and realized that we were in the midst of the overwintering monarchs, occurring in such dense clusters that they vividly altered the appearance of the forest. Our first impressions were overwhelming, not only because of the incredible numbers of

butterflies assembled in one location but also because of the profound biological implications of the phenomenon.

As Dr. Brower and his team stepped carefully underneath the towering oyamel trees that were cloaked in monarch butterflies, who should they encounter but Dr. Fred and Norah Urquhart! They had been sitting among the monarchs, tagging as many as they could. Imagine how shocked everyone must have been, to run into one another in the exact place that Dr. Urquhart had been trying to keep secret. Dr. Brower later wrote,

FIGURE 4-2. Lincoln Brower (standing with his left hand on his hip) confronting Dr. Fred Urquhart (sitting and wearing a hat) at the Sierra Chincua site, January 22, 1977.

"The Urquharts were bewildered by our arrival and initially treated us rudely, and then with hostility."

After what must have been an uncomfortable conversation, the Urquharts continued their tagging, and Dr. Brower and his team went off to explore the site. At one point, unbeknownst to Dr. Brower, one of the Mexican guides, feeling a chill, had built a bonfire. The heat from the bonfire warmed the butterflies that hung from the trees above, and millions of them fell to the ground. Dr. Brower rushed over and told the guide to put out the fire. But it was too late. A thick layer of monarchs surrounded a tripod that Dr. Brower had set up to videotape birds that were feeding on the butterflies. Now that the monarchs were on the ground, no longer snug in the trees, they might not warm up enough in the cold air to be able to fly back to the safety of the tree trunks and branches. Dr. Brower was devastated. To make matters worse, who should witness the commotion? Norah Urquhart!

Norah must have stood in dismay, staring at all the fallen butterflies. She saw the tripod standing in the middle of the scene. Dr. Brower later wrote that she accused him of lighting fires under the butterflies "to dislodge monarchs from their roosting trees to provide material for dramatic photographic shots." Dr. Brower could not convince her that what had happened was an innocent mistake. The Urquharts later mailed a "special report" to their research associates that told how Dr. Brower and his team followed Trail and Brugger to the site and started lighting fires. Dr. Brower wrote to Dr. Urquhart, explaining in detail how he and his team had found the Sierra Chincua site on their own, and that the Urquharts had misinterpreted their research activities. Dr. Brower wrote: "The Urquharts never replied either to this or to any of several other attempts to reconcile the situation."

In the end, Dr. Brower decided not to publicly respond to the accusations the Urquharts made, which had spread throughout the scientific community. "In retrospect," said Dr. Brower, "this was a mistake, because the unrefuted allegations polarized the monarch community—the very group of people who, had they adopted a unified front, could have been far more effective at promoting conservation of the overwintering sites."

As we will see, Dr. Brower continued to study the monarchs at the Mexican overwintering sites as well as their predators and the special climate of the forests. What he and his team discovered became crucial to our understanding of both the biology and survival of the eastern monarch butterfly.

## CHAPTER FIVE

# SECRETS OF THE FOREST

What an incredible sight for Dr. Brower and his team to see at Sierra Chincua: branches and trunks of oyamel trees completely covered in monarch butterflies, clustered close together like pages in a book. But looking down at the ground, Dr. Brower saw things that also sparked his interest. Not only were dead monarch butterflies scattered all over, but many of the dead bodies were mangled in some way. They had tattered wings, partially eaten **abdomens**, and some bodies didn't even have a head! It was a rather gruesome sight. Obviously, something was attacking the butterflies. After watching the trees for a while, Dr. Brower spotted the culprits: two types of birds, black-backed orioles and black-headed grosbeaks. They swooped in and attacked the clusters of monarchs in the trees, pecking at them and dropping uneaten parts onto Dr. Brower's head below. Two questions popped into his mind: How many monarch butterflies were these birds killing at Sierra Chincua? And how could the birds eat the monarchs if the monarchs were filled with poisonous cardenolides? As a scientist, Dr. Brower wanted to figure out the answers.

First, Dr. Brower and his team suspended over eighty big nets, each three feet by three feet square, about six and a half feet off the ground. At the end of each day, between 4:00 and 6:30 p.m., they counted what they called "butterfly items" that had fallen into the nets: dead or dying butterflies with parts of their bodies eaten, heads, **thoraxes**, abdomens, dismembered wings, and bodies with zero to four wings still attached. Dr. Brower and his team estimated that black-backed orioles and black-headed grosbeaks killed about 15,067 butterflies on average *per day*. During the 135-day overwintering season, that amounted to about 2 million butterflies. However, that was only about 9 percent of the entire overwintering colony. So, yes, birds at the Sierra Chincua overwintering site do eat a lot of monarch butterflies. But at the time, in the early 1980s, the colonies of butterflies were so huge that it amounted only to a small fraction of the roosting population.

Next, Dr. Brower and his team used binoculars to watch the birds feeding on the monarchs. The birds had different strategies to get at the rich, fatty innards of the butterflies while avoiding the poisonous wings and **exoskeleton**. Black-backed orioles pinned down the monarch butterflies with their feet, sliced open the abdomen with their beak, and then ate the fatty, nutritious guts. They didn't eat any of the wings or exoskeleton. When they were done, they tossed the remains of the butterfly to the ground. Black-headed grosbeaks, on the other hand, used their beak to rip off the butterfly's wings. Then they ate the entire body whole!

It's quite incredible that two different species of birds figured out how to avoid getting sick while eating monarch butterflies. However, black-backed orioles and black-headed grosbeaks were not the only predators of monarch butterflies at the Sierra Chincua overwintering site.

## HIDDEN WINGS

Dr. Brower and his team also found little piles of monarch butterfly wings hidden beneath logs and plants. What kind of critter was stashing butterfly wings? To find out, in the evening, they set up box-shaped live traps baited with what they hoped were tasty morsels: rolled oats, peanut butter, and sunflower seeds. The next morning, they checked the traps. What was inside? Mice! To be absolutely certain that the mice were

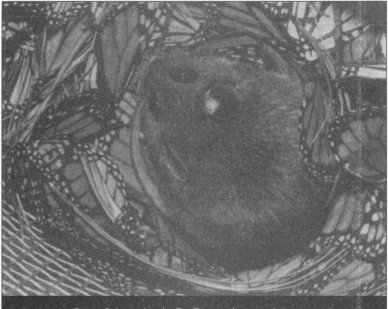

*FIGURE 5-1.* One of the mice in Dr. Brower's experiment made a nest out of the uneaten remains of the monarch butterflies she was fed.

feeding on the monarchs, they had to examine the mice's stomach contents. So, they humanely killed the mice with chloroform, which is a toxic gas that in high enough doses can kill, and they opened up the mice's stomachs. They found the food that was used to lure the mice, and they found scales from monarch butterfly wings, small pieces of monarch exoskeleton, abdominal fat, and **trachea** (breathing tubes). Mice were indeed feeding on monarch butterflies at Sierra Chincua. Dr. Brower and his team then placed some mice in cages and offered them some monarch butterflies. Like the birds, mice ate the thoraxes and abdomens, mostly sucking out the insides.

Dr. Brower and his team estimated that mice probably eat between 330 to 2,400 butterflies per day at the Sierra Chincua site. Like the birds, they do not pose a significant danger to the survival of monarch butterflies as a species.

One of Dr. Brower's main motives for visiting the Sierra Chincua overwintering site was to study **predation** on monarch butterflies. But as he wandered around, marveling at the millions upon millions of monarchs roosting in the mountain's oyamel trees, Dr. Brower also wondered, *Why here?* Why did the monarchs choose year after year to journey to these remote forests in

Michoacán to rest for the winter? To answer these questions, Dr. Brower's team next studied the **microclimate** of the Sierra Chincua overwintering site—the temperature, wind, and precipitation of where the butterflies roost that differs from that of the surrounding area.

### THE GOOD THAT CAME FROM STORMS

Dr. Brower and his team continued to go to the Sierra Chincua overwintering site every year to do their research. By the early 1980s, they noticed that during two of the five seasons they had been there, the ground was covered up to six inches deep with dead butterflies. That's a lot of dead monarchs. Did the birds go on a binge? Closer inspection suggested no. Although they were dead, the butterflies were in perfect shape. They were not mangled or wounded, which would be expected if they had been killed by birds. What could have killed so many butterflies without even a scratch? After camping at Sierra Chincua in January 1981, the team had their answer: winter storms.

On January 13, 1981, the storms began. Cold temperatures descended on the area. Rain and hail soaked the butterfly clusters every day. Snow started falling four days later, and it kept falling for three days.

Branches, weighed down with soaked butterflies and snow, started breaking off trees. It was too cold for the fallen butterflies to climb back up another tree, and many were trapped on the ground under the snow. Then there were two days of calm, when the rain and snow stopped but the temperature stayed below freezing. It was still too cold for the fallen butterflies to fly to safety, and they became even further trapped with the freezing of the snow's surface. On January 22, the butterflies were slammed with yet another storm. More wet snow blanketed the already soaked branches and butterfly clusters. More butterfly-covered branches fell, the tops of some trees broke off, and one tree was completely uprooted. Finally, early in the morning of January 24, the sky cleared. The storms stopped. However, it was still extremely cold, with temperatures around 24 degrees Fahrenheit.

Butterflies fell from the trees for days. Dr. Brower wrote that they "plummeted to the ground like inanimate objects." The clusters of butterflies on the trees looked thinned out. To get a sense of how many butterflies fell after the storm, Dr. Brower and his team spread out tarps under some trees. Imagine an area that is divided into squares, with each square being ten feet by ten feet. During an earlier part of the storm, the rate of falling butterflies was only one butterfly per square per hour. Two days after the storms ended, an incredible eighty-eight butterflies fell in each of these squares *per hour*. The poor butterflies were still suffering greatly two days after the storms had ended. It was likely the cold temperatures following the storms that killed them.

The team did an experiment to test the effects of cold temperatures on the monarchs' ability to fly. They

**FIGURE 5-2.** Dead or almost-dead butterflies on the ground under a tree after the storms of January 1981. The thermometer in the pile of butterflies is about ten inches high.

took samples of butterflies from tree branches, tree trunks, low plants, and directly off the ground. They put the butterflies in nylon-mesh cages in the sun and let the butterflies warm up for about two hours. Then they released the butterflies one by one and categorized them as: (1) dead, (2) almost dead (unable to fly but showed some sign of life), (3) flew but landed about fifty feet away, and (4) flew off normally. Butterflies that were collected from the ground after the storms were often dead or close to dying. Butterflies that were sampled from higher up in tree branches and tree trunks were much more likely to be flight impaired or normal. The trees seemed to provide safety from the storms.

If roosting in the trees gives monarch butterflies protection, why do so many monarchs hang out in low-lying plants and on the ground? Dr. Brower and his team saw that when the sun came out during the day and the air warmed up to about 55 degrees Fahrenheit, the monarchs were able to fly. A number of monarchs would leave their tree branches or tree trunks to get a drink of water from nearby dew, puddles, or freshwater streams. If the air stayed warm, the butterflies could fly back to their roosts. If the air cooled, however, the butterflies could no longer fly and they might have made a pit stop on the ground or on plants until the sun warmed them enough to fly again. If a storm developed while they were on or near the ground, they're trapped there until it subsides. As Dr. Brower and his team discovered, these butterflies can die if they become covered in rain, snow, or ice. They may also just end up freezing to death. Leaving the roosts for a drink is a risky move, because nice weather might turn bad before they can return to the safety of the trees.

The storms of January 1981 killed about 2.5 million monarch butterflies at Sierra Chincua. That is a phenomenal number of dead monarchs. However, there were so many millions of butterflies in the colony to begin with that although the storm thinned out the tree clusters and blanketed the ground with dead and dying bodies, there were, thankfully, plenty of butterflies left in the spring to ensure the survival of the next generation.

Despite the deadly storms, a lot of good information was uncovered. Dr. Brower and his team learned that if monarch butterflies are just a little bit wet from the rain or snow and they are not in the safety of the trees, about half of them will die if the temperature falls to 24 degrees Fahrenheit. On the other hand, if butterflies remain dry in the trees, they can withstand temperatures as low as 17 degrees Fahrenheit. What is it about the trees that make them a safe haven for the butterflies? These were questions that Dr. Brower and his team pursued next.

## SLINGSHOTS AND SWEET SPOTS

Curiously, the thickest monarch butterfly clusters were always found partway up the tall oyamel fir trees. Why did the monarchs prefer to hang out in the middle? Dr. Brower and his team had a hunch that the butterflies had found the warmest and coziest part of the trees. To confirm this, they needed to measure the air temperature at the top of the trees, the middle of the trees, and the bottom of the trees. Measuring the air temperature at the bottom of the trees was not a problem. They could reach that. But how could they measure the air temperature midway up and at the treetop? The oyamel firs were over seventy feet high. The answer? A high-powered slingshot!

The team used tiny, button-shaped devices called **thermochrons** that accurately record temperature every hour. The thermochrons were smaller than an inch, so the team put each one inside a PVC tube to protect it. Then they attached the tube to a nylon string, put the tube into a slingshot, and *ZING-O!* They shot the tube with the thermochron up, up, up into the trees. The tubes hung suspended from the branches where the thermochron inside could record the temperature. They aimed some tubes so that they hung partway up the trees, and other tubes were shot up and over the trees to measure the temperature at the very top. The highest they were able to shoot the tubes was about seventy-two feet.

After the tubes dangled up in the trees for around twenty-four days, they reeled them in and downloaded the data onto a computer. Their hunch was confirmed: The air temperature partway up the trees tended to be slightly warmer, especially during cold nights, compared to the tops and the bottoms. When the sun was out and the air was warm, the air partway up the trees was actually a bit cooler. This is important because the slightly cooler temperatures would prevent the butterflies from burning their stored fat, allowing them to survive the long winter. The butterflies seemed to be hanging out in the sweet spot in the trees. But air temperature was also affected by how close the trees were to one another. Trees in more dense parts of the forest tended to be warmer for the butterflies, whereas trees that were more spaced apart tended to be cooler. Tree size was also a factor: The bigger the tree, the warmer it was compared to the forest air. It was crystal clear to Dr. Brower and his team the importance of protecting the oyamel firs from logging, especially the bigger, older trees.

## PRO MONARCA

Dr. Brower and his team were not the only ones who learned how important the forests were for monarch butterflies. After reading Dr. Urquhart's story in *National Geographic*, a lawyer in Mexico City named Rodolfo Ogarrio decided to take a trip to Sierra Chincua to see the overwintering monarch colonies. In January 1977, he saw the butterfly-covered trees for himself. He marveled that such a natural spectacle occurred each year not far from his own home. To his surprise, on that trip he ran into the Urquharts and Dr. Brower!

Ogarrio realized that it was only a matter of time before tourists began flooding the overwintering grounds. Inspired by his experience in the forest and with the help of Mexico City engineer Fernando Ortíz Monasterio, he founded the nonprofit organization Pro Mariposa Monarca, also known as Pro Monarca. The aim of Pro Monarca was to protect the sites where monarch butterflies overwinter and, in Ogarrio's words, "to bring together members of various institutions that share a common interest, independently of whether they belong to the government, scientific, or private sector, and whether they be Mexicans or foreigners." Pro Monarca began lobbying the Mexican government to establish a protected area in Michoacán.

## SOLVING A SPRINGTIME MYSTERY

As we've learned, Dr. Brower spent many winters in the mountains of Michoacán where monarch butterflies roost in the trees. But spring was also on his mind. In March, the weather becomes warmer and the sun stays out longer. The millions of monarchs clustered in the trees take flight, drink water from streams, and mate before beginning the long journey north to the United States and southern Canada. By late May and June, monarchs can be spotted in northern US states such as Wisconsin, Minnesota, Pennsylvania, and Michigan, and in southern Ontario, Canada. Some scientists believed that monarchs are strong enough to fly all the way up to these places. The butterflies then lay their eggs for the next generation and die. This is called the

**single sweep hypothesis**: The monarchs return "home" to the northern United States and southern Canada in one long trip or "swoop."

Other scientists argued that the long flight back north to these areas would be too much for a butterfly, especially after it had spent a winter in the Mexican mountains. The monarchs would run out of steam. These scientists proposed that instead, starting in March, the overwintering monarchs fly only as far as Texas and Louisiana. They lay their eggs and die. The new generation of monarchs that grow from these eggs would then continue the journey northward. These butterflies also lay eggs along the way, and this next generation keeps going. As a result, it is actually the grandchildren of the overwintering monarchs that finally make it to the northern United States and southern Canada. Scientists called this the **successive brood hypothesis**, because it takes successive generations (or broods) for monarchs to repopulate the north each year.

Dr. Brower was intrigued. Which hypothesis was true, the single sweep hypothesis or the successive brood hypothesis? He and his colleagues, the husband-and-wife team of Dr. Stephen Malcolm and Dr. Barbara Cockrell, set out to solve this mystery.

It would have been nice to follow the monarchs as they left the Mexican mountains in March and made their way north. But if you've ever tried to follow a butterfly on foot, or even on a bike or by car, you know how difficult this is. Instead, the three scientists designed a very clever, three-step experiment.

After collecting over 1,000 monarch butterflies across the southern and northern United States between March and June, they rated the amount of wing wear on each butterfly. They used a five-point scale, where 1 was for wings in perfect condition and 5 was for wings that were extremely worn—missing scales, faded, torn, and frayed. Monarchs collected from the southern United States had wings that were quite worn. They were faded, tattered, and had missing scales. Monarchs from the northern United States, however, had wings that were in perfect condition, suggesting they were brand-new adult butterflies. This finding supports the successive brood hypothesis.

Next, Dr. Brower, Dr. Malcolm, and Dr. Cockrell knew that the concentration of cardenolides in a monarch butterfly fades over time. They froze and ground up the butterflies (poor monarchs!), and then analyzed the amount of cardenolides that was in their bodies. Monarchs from Mexico and the southern United States showed rather low levels of cardenolides, suggesting they were older monarch butterflies. Monarchs from the northern United States had, on average, twice the amount of cardenolides, suggesting they were a younger population. Another point for the successive brood hypothesis.

For the final experiment, the team used the cardenolide fingerprinting technique that we learned about earlier. They found that monarchs from the overwintering grounds and southern United States had fingerprints that matched those from common milkweed. The monarchs from the northern United States, however, mostly had fingerprints that matched a different type of milkweed: green milkweed. Therefore, butterflies from the northern United States fed on different milkweed as caterpillars and are of a different generation. Yet more support for the successive brood hypothesis.

All three experiments pointed to the successive brood hypothesis as the likely way that monarch butterflies repopulate the United States and southern Canada in spring. Thus, in March, after mating among the oyamel fir trees where they had roosted for the winter, monarchs make their way to southern states such as Texas and Louisiana, lay eggs, and then die. It is the offspring that then continue their way north.

## A CHAMPION FOR MONARCHS

Over time, after Dr. Brower and his team began their research at Sierra Chincua, other monarch butterfly overwintering sites were found. Until the mid-1990s, the only site open to tourism was El Rosario, and the tourism was managed by Pro Monarca. The Alliance of Ejidos and Communities of the Monarch Butterfly Reserve protested, asking that the Mexican government open more sites. These included Cerro Pelón, Piedra Herrada, and Sierra Chincua. As we will see later, the area in Mexico

FIGURE 5-3. Dr. Lincoln Brower.

containing most of the overwintering sites has been designated the Monarch Butterfly Biosphere Reserve. Dr. Brower became extremely involved in conservation work for all the overwintering sites.

Dr. Brower and his team propelled our knowledge to new heights about monarch butterflies, their predators, and the special climate of the Mexican overwintering sites. They showed how important the oyamel forests in the Trans-Mexican Volcanic Belt are to monarch butterfly survival. And finally, they unlocked the mystery of how monarchs repopulate North America in the spring: Successive generations of monarchs lay eggs farther and farther north until they reach southern Canada. In addition, thanks to his work with barfing blue jays, he is known as one of the fathers of the field of **chemical ecology**: the study of how organisms interact with their environment through naturally occurring chemicals. Known as the Champion of Monarchs, Dr. Brower passed away in 2018 at the age of eighty-six.

As we will see in the next chapter, much work started by Dr. Brower and his team to track monarchs is continuing, thanks to advances in technology and the curiosity of people like you and me.

## CHAPTER SIX

# TRACKING MIGRATION

Dr. Fred and Norah Urquhart, Dr. Lincoln Brower, and their respective teams worked tirelessly to understand the biology and behavior of monarch butterflies. Picking up where they left off were two scientists in particular, Dr. Orley "Chip" Taylor, of Monarch Watch, and Elizabeth Howard, of Journey North. They have continued the tradition of tracking monarchs during their migration and involving the public. Their work has given us an even closer look at the amazing travels of monarch butterflies.

## MONARCH WATCH

In the early 1990s, Dr. Taylor was scheduled to teach a course at the University of Kansas on experimental field biology. He needed a group or class project for the students. What would the students find interesting? What subject matter would be easy for them to study? An animal? A plant? He pondered the matter for a while as he stepped through the long grass at one of his field sites. Then he saw a flash of orange out of the corner of his eye. He turned to see a monarch butterfly perched on a wildflower. That got him thinking. *What about monarch butterflies?*

Dr. Taylor knew that each fall, multitudes of monarchs fly through the area around the university on their way to Mexico for the winter. Students would have a great time catching and studying them. He thought about possible questions students could answer about monarch butterflies within class time, and he read as much as he could. He soon came across the work published by the Urquharts, describing their tagging efforts to discover where monarchs go in the fall. By then the locations of the monarchs' Mexican overwintering grounds were no longer a secret, but Dr. Taylor had questions that the Urquharts hadn't answered. For instance, how do monarchs know when to start migrating? As they migrate, do they fly at a steady speed along the entire journey, or do they speed up or slow down at certain points?

Tagging monarchs similar to how the Urquharts had done it might help answer these questions. And like scientists before him, Dr. Taylor recognized that if they were going to tag monarchs, they would need help from the public. "So, as a venture, a gamble really, to determine if we could learn more about the migration through tagging, we sent out two press releases," Dr. Taylor said. "One press release was in Iowa and the other was in Texas, asking for volunteers to tag monarchs during the migration." He received over 1,000 responses. The feedback was tremendous, especially from teachers. "The success of this outreach led to the founding of Monarch Watch in 1992," said Dr. Taylor.

Since then, over 10,000 volunteers across southern Canada and the midwestern United States have tagged over 2 million monarch butterflies. Each fall, Monarch Watch mails out more than a quarter of a million tags to volunteers. The program has been, and continues to be, a huge success. How does it work? If you live east of the Rocky Mountains, you can order tags from monarchwatch.org. They are mailed to you, along with detailed tagging instructions, in late summer or early fall. Each tag has a unique code made up of numbers and letters (see Figure 6-1). Once your butterfly is tagged, you email the tag's code, date, location of the tagging, whether the monarch was male or female, and your contact information to Monarch Watch so they can enter the details into their database. (The Urquharts never had the luxury of email!) If the monarch you tagged is later recovered, Monarch Watch will contact you.

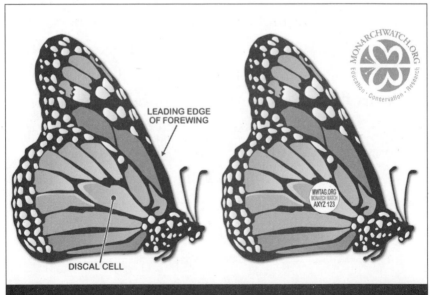

**FIGURE 6-1.** Placement of a Monarch Watch tag on a monarch butterfly. The tag is placed on the discal cell of the wing. Each tag has a unique code made up of letters and numbers.

One goal of Monarch Watch is for people to find and report tagged monarchs *after* they have been released. Hopefully, tagged monarchs will be seen again by someone along the butterflies' migratory route or when they are at one of the overwintering sites in Mexico. Whoever finds a tagged butterfly can go to monarchwatch.org to enter the butterfly's special code and the date and location where it was seen.

Interestingly, most recovered Monarch Watch tags are found at the Mexican overwintering sites. Usually, tour guides and Mexican locals find dead, tagged butterflies on the ground, under the roosting colonies, or on trails. Monarch Watch sends representatives to Mexico to collect the tags and pay the people who find them.

People have been sending Dr. Taylor and his team monarch tag recovery data since 1992, and now the database is huge. Dr. Taylor has started to look for patterns in the data to see what more we can learn about the yearly monarch migration.

As we saw earlier, one question Dr. Taylor had was about the **pace** of travel of the monarchs as they fly to Mexico. A number of scientists believed that weather was a factor. If monarchs run into bad weather, such as rain or strong winds, they would slow down or even have to make a pit stop until the weather improves. Also, if it is too hot or too cold, monarchs won't fly. A cold spell of 55 degrees Fahrenheit or lower, or a heat wave of 86 degrees Fahrenheit or higher, will certainly slow their progress. The butterflies would have to wait until flying conditions are more favorable. And when weather is good, maybe they speed up a bit. Who knows?

Dr. Taylor wondered if the pace of the monarch migration might be affected by a cue from the sun, called the **sun angle at solar noon** (SASN for short). What is the SASN? We know the sun moves across the sky throughout the day. As it moves, the angle between the sun and the ground changes. The angle is biggest halfway between sunrise and sunset at solar noon (see Figure 6-2). But the angle is not always the same each day at noon: It changes with the seasons, and it depends what latitude you're at.

Dr. Taylor and his team dug into the Monarch Watch data. They noticed that some people from Winnipeg, Canada—one of the most northern tagging locations—reported that monarchs started flying south in early August, when the SASN is 57 degrees. Monarchs arrive at the overwintering sites in Mexico at the end of October, when the SASN is again 57 degrees. Is 57

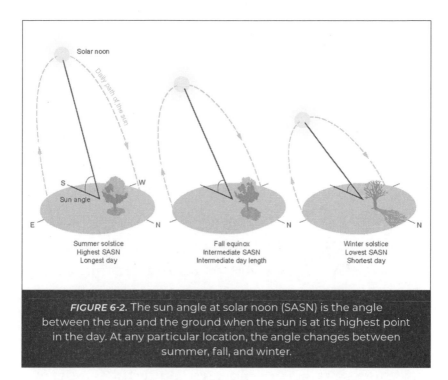

**Solar noon**

Daily path of the sun

S
W
Sun angle
E
N

N

N

| Summer solstice | Fall equinox | Winter solstice |
| Highest SASN | Intermediate SASN | Lowest SASN |
| Longest day | Intermediate day length | Shortest day |

**FIGURE 6-2.** The sun angle at solar noon (SASN) is the angle between the sun and the ground when the sun is at its highest point in the day. At any particular location, the angle changes between summer, fall, and winter.

the magic number? Do monarchs travel at a pace that allows them to follow a SASN of 57 degrees? To find out, Dr. Taylor and his team examined the tagging and recovery data from their database. They calculated the general daily movement rates of the butterflies as they made their way to Mexico. Then they figured out the rates that would be expected if the monarchs were following a SASN of 57 degrees. It was a match! But it wasn't quite a perfect match. Monarchs might adjust the pace of their migration to maintain a constant velocity. They might also try to fly at a rate so that they are always in places where the temperature is a comfy 68 to 86 degrees Fahrenheit.

Overall, the pace of the monarch migration appears to be slow-fast-slow: slow near the beginning, speeding up near the midway point of their trip, and then slowing down again as they near Mexico.

Thanks to over thirty years' worth of tagging and recovery data from volunteers across North America, Monarch Watch was able to help reveal this secret behind the pacing of the monarch butterfly migration. The data can also show us how we might direct our conservation efforts. Over the years, scientists have taken measurements at the Monarch Butterfly Biosphere Reserve and have found that the monarch butterfly population is shrinking. (We'll talk more about this in Chapter Ten.) Scientists identified two possible explanations. One is the **milkweed limitation hypothesis**. This hypothesis suggests that much less milkweed is available in the monarch breeding areas for female monarchs to lay their eggs. Fewer eggs mean fewer monarchs ending up in Mexico. Why is the amount of milkweed shrinking? To answer this question, we need to step back for a moment and look at certain agricultural practices.

For years, people have been transforming vast areas of natural land into crops, mainly corn and soybean fields. In the 1970s, to make sure only corn and soybeans grew in these fields, the product Roundup was invented. Roundup is the brand name given to **glyphosate**. Glyphosate is an **herbicide**, which is a chemical that kills unwanted plants and grasses.[10] Then, in the 1990s, scientists managed to genetically engineer corn and soybean plants so that they didn't die when Roundup was sprayed on them. These plants are referred to as glyphosate-resistant, or "Roundup Ready." Farmers who planted Roundup Ready seeds could now spray Roundup over their corn and soybean crops to get rid of unwanted weeds and plants without damaging the corn and soybeans. This increased the trend of **monocultures**: large expanses of land where only one type of crop or plant grows. (Tidy-looking lawns and golf courses can also be considered monocultures.) Monocultures offer

---

10. These unwanted grasses and plants are often referred to as **weeds**. "Weeds" can actually be plants that play a big role in the ecosystem. For instance, some wildflowers are considered weeds, but they feed pollinating insects. Milkweed is considered a weed (especially given the last part of its name), but they're the only plant on which monarchs can lay their eggs and monarch caterpillars can grow. Is there really such a thing as a weed, a plant that is only a pest and provides no benefit whatsoever to the ecosystem? Something to think about.

monarch butterflies and other pollinators very little or no nutrition, and for that reason they are considered "food deserts."

Over time, more and more land was converted to agriculture, and the use of glyphosate exploded. In the United States, there are over 750 products for sale that contain glyphosate. In 2014, about 26.7 *million* pounds of glyphosate were used across the country. This is approximately the weight of six fully loaded NASA space shuttles. Today, over 90 percent of the land used to grow corn and soybeans is occupied by genetically engineered, herbicide-resistant corn and soybeans.

This spelled disaster for milkweed. It is one of the "unwanted" plants that takes up space in corn and soybean fields. As farmers treated their crops with glyphosate, milkweed quickly disappeared. For example, in 1999, in Iowa alone, milkweed was found in 51 percent of corn and soybean fields; by 2009, it was found in only 8 percent of the fields. One estimate was that by 2006 about 61 million acres of land across the midwestern United States no longer had milkweed. That's roughly the size of 61 million football fields.

Returning to the milkweed limitation hypothesis, it suggests we should plant and preserve more milkweed so that female monarchs have more area in which to lay their eggs.

On the other hand, the **migration mortality hypothesis** suggests that the overwintering population is a lot smaller now because more and more monarchs are dying as they make their way south to Mexico. They can be killed in three ways. One is by not eating enough nectar because there are fewer flowers available, so they starve to death or don't store enough fat to allow them to survive the winter. Another way they can die is by falling victim to parasites that make them sick. Finally, monarchs can be hit or run over by traffic as they cross roadways.

If the migration mortality hypothesis is true, then it implies that we should funnel our energy toward planting more wildflowers, controlling parasites that make monarchs sick, and figuring out how monarchs can cross roadways safely. These are very different conservation strategies compared to planting and preserving milkweed. It's worth our while to figure out which hypothesis better represents what's going on with the monarch population.

The team at Monarch Watch realized they could use the tagging and recovery data submitted by volunteers to help shed light on the issue. By studying the data in their database, they found a rather strong relationship between the number of monarchs that were tagged each late summer and early fall and the number of recovered tags in Mexico. In other words, large summer populations of monarchs were related to large overwintering populations. This is predicted by the milkweed limitation hypothesis. (The monarch mortality hypothesis predicts larger summer populations and smaller overwintering populations because many monarchs die on their way to Mexico.)

At this point, Monarch Watch has found more support for the milkweed limitation hypothesis. But this is not to say that monarchs don't die during their migration to the Mexican overwintering sites. Many do, and many die because of the things predicted by the migration mortality hypothesis. It's just that the milkweed limitation hypothesis appears to be a better predictor of what is going on. We must keep in mind, however, that Monarch Watch data includes only data from monarchs that were tagged, and people can't tag every single monarch. Although this technically makes Monarch Watch data incomplete, it is still extremely useful. And it may become even more useful over time, with better technology and better mathematical methods.

One thing the Monarch Watch team included in their analyses was a measure of the "greenness" of areas in the midwestern United States. Greenness means how many available nectar sources (flowers) the monarchs would encounter on their way to Mexico. Greenness did in fact partially predict the size of the overwintering populations. So, perhaps the migration mortality hypothesis is not entirely wrong: lack of flowers could drive the death of monarchs before they reach their winter destination. That's one cool thing about science: Sometimes things are not strictly black and white, with one hypothesis wrong and the other right. Sometimes the explanation is a bit of both—a shade of gray.

Overall, thanks to Monarch Watch data (contributed by people like you and me) and the work of the Monarch Watch team, we've learned that one thing we can do to help the monarchs is to plant and preserve milkweed, and plant and preserve wildflowers, too. What other discoveries are waiting to be made with all the Monarch Watch data? As Dr. Taylor pointed out, he and his team have only begun to scratch the surface.

There is now even more complexity behind the decline in the monarch butterfly population. In 2021, a group of scientists from the United States and Mexico published a study showing that climate change is having negative impacts on the numbers of monarch butterflies. They found that since 2004, monarch breeding season weather has been the most important factor affecting the size of the monarch population. Herbicide use, milkweed loss, and mortality during the fall migration are still having an impact on the butterflies, but spring and summer weather conditions are now having the biggest effects. More specifically, temperatures are rising, particularly in lower latitudes where monarchs breed. If temperatures continue to rise, scientists predict it will become too hot for monarchs to breed successfully.

The decline in the monarch butterfly population is truly a challenging problem. Slowing climate change is not as easy or quick as planting more milkweed and ending herbicide use. On the other hand, the impact on monarch butterflies and their spectacular fall migration are more reasons why we must address the global problem of climate change.

## JOURNEY NORTH

Growing up in Minnesota, Elizabeth Howard was always excited when spring came. She loved the arrival of the songbirds each year. As a kid she would telephone the Rare Bird Alert hotlines that were organized by local Audubon Society members. People could call these hotlines and report their bird sightings. Howard often called the hotlines of the more southern states, such as Texas, to ask whether songbirds had been sighted. If they had, Howard knew it was only a matter of time before they made it up north to where she lived.

In the early 1990s, when Howard was an adult, she read a book by Edwin Way Teale called *North with the Spring*. It is a true story about how Teale and his wife, Nellie, drove north from Florida to witness the unfolding of spring across the country. Howard was so inspired by *North with the Spring* that she wanted to figure out a way to share the wonders of spring migrations with kids across the country. Then she heard about a trans-Antarctica dogsled expedition led by Will Steger. He used radio to communicate while he was in Antarctica, and then his messages were spread to different parts of the world by the internet and email. At the time, both the internet and email were relatively new, and most people didn't use them daily (or even have them) the way we do now.

Howard thought about the notion that people could send emails to one another. A vision formed in her mind of a computer screen showing a map of North America. Dots popped up on the map where people had reported sightings of migrating animals. Songbirds, humming-birds, monarch butterflies . . . If people reported a sighting, they could see their own sighting as one of the dots on the map. The map could act as a sort of story-telling so kids in schools around the country could see how the ecosystem and food chain rebuild in the spring. If they looked outside their window, they might see snow and ice, but they could see reports from other children in more southern areas showing where they already had milkweed and flowers and warm temperatures. All the kids could feel like they were a part of the story of the unfolding of spring. At the same time, they could learn about how where they live fits in with wildlife migrations.

Howard set to work, and before long, the pieces fell into place. Howard and her team developed a way for members of the public to send messages about sightings of migrating animals. Each sighting appeared as a dot on a map. Her vision came true! Teachers across the country were eager to have their students join in. As a tribute to Teale's book that inspired her, Howard called her new program Journey North.

Kids' and teachers' sightings of migrating animals started to pour in. However, it was difficult to get information from Mexico because the phone lines weren't great and not many people at Journey North spoke Spanish, so it took a long time to explain their work. "But the message we did finally get was from one of Dr. Lincoln Brower's graduate students who was at the overwintering site," Howard recalled. "It was sort of an announcement of 'Here they come!' For sure that was my favorite message, or sighting, that we ever got."

Fast-forward to today. Journey North is flourishing, with sightings pouring in each year not only from students and teachers but from members of the public across North America. The website, journeynorth.org, provides maps and information about a variety of animals, including monarch butterflies, birds, frogs, and whales. It tracks many signs of spring, such as when leaves begin growing on trees and when ice starts melting from rivers, lakes, ponds, and oceans.

"Technology-wise," Howard said, "we have changed Journey North over time by keeping up with the amazing technical advances that have grown exponentially since we began. We had a text-only website as early as 1995. We incorporated images and video clips increasingly over the years, as quickly as bandwidth allowed. Later, we incorporated a real-time database, live maps, and user-submitted images." Howard is most proud of how Journey North tells the story of the monarch butterfly migration by using real-time observations people make across the butterflies' migration route. "When people report the emergence of milkweed and the arrival of the first monarchs," said Howard, "they see the importance and relevance of the habitat they are creating and/or preserving for monarchs."

Journey North has now existed for over twenty-five years. It was a pioneer in online **citizen science**, before people actually started calling it citizen science. (Citizen science is the public's contribution of observations and data to scientific projects and research led by scientists. Monarch Watch and the Urquharts' tagging program are also examples of citizen science.)

Today, teachers across North America continue to send Journey North sightings of monarchs, other migrating animals, and other signs of spring. But lots of sightings now come from families and individuals from the public, like you and me. Over time, Howard and others working behind the scenes at Journey North began to realize the scientific potential of the program. With thousands of people sending monarch sightings each year, they now had a huge database of monarch butterfly migration behavior.

Howard and her team started asking questions. What was the first state where people began seeing monarchs in the spring? What states followed? The team looked at five years' worth of sighting data and discovered that monarchs were nearly always reported from Texas first, followed usually by Louisiana or Florida. Next is often Mississippi, followed by Arkansas and Oklahoma. The migration then continues northward across a broad front, probably mostly by the offspring of the monarchs that originally left Mexico. The Canadian provinces were always last (except Ontario, which is shown as 23 furtherest to the left on the map in Figure 6-3).

Thanks to Journey North, scientists can explore questions they weren't able to before. For instance, when does the monarch spring migration begin? How long does it take for monarch butterflies to spread

**FIGURE 6-3.** The order in which monarch butterflies were seen in each state or province during their spring migration, based on five years of Journey North data.

out across the United States and Canada during their spring migration? Howard and her team again looked at five years' worth of sighting data. They found no consistent patterns. The timing and duration of the monarch spring migration tends to vary from year to year. Why is this so? Perhaps it depends on weather conditions each spring. Perhaps it depends on when milkweed emerges after the winter thaw. Maybe it is both. Or maybe there are other factors at play. These are all questions that remain to be answered.

As we saw earlier, the size of the overwintering colonies in Mexico is shrinking. (We'll read more about this in Chapter Ten.) Howard and her friend Dr. Andrew Davis, who is a scientist at the University of Georgia, wondered, *Is the spring migration north shrinking, too?* They looked at the Journey North data and found that the date of the first spring sightings of monarchs had been shifting at a rate of about one day later every four years. This trend was not a result of the number of people submitting data to Journey North, nor was it a result of when milkweed began to emerge in the spring. The later sightings could be a result of fewer butterflies. Howard and Dr. Davis also discovered that over the eighteen years of Journey North data, the **range** of the locations of monarch sightings decreased by about 9 percent. That's quite alarming. However, near the end of the spring migration each year—around the end of April— the range of monarch butterfly sightings *didn't* change. So, even though the Mexican overwintering colonies were becoming smaller, and the monarchs might not spread out as much as they travel north in the spring, they end up populating the same amount of land in the United States and Canada.

We must keep in mind that Journey North data, as valuable as it is, is based on people's *sightings* of monarch butterflies. This is not the same as knowing the actual number of monarch butterflies that exist. For instance, Journey North can tell us the range or total area where monarchs were seen and recorded, but how many monarchs are actually within that area? Unfortunately, the data can't tell us that. But at least it is a huge step in the right direction. With future technology, what will Journey North look like in five years? Ten years? Maybe someone reading this book (even you!) might have a hand in that.

## MONARCH BUTTERFLY REST STOPS

Have you ever been on a long car trip? If you have, chances are at some point you needed to stop at a rest stop for a bathroom break, a snack, or to put more gas in your car or recharge your electric car. During their long journey to Mexico in the fall, monarch butterflies make pit stops, too. They often settle on trees or bushes for the night since they can't fly in the dark and they need a chance to rest. Sometimes, a large group of monarchs gather together and form a tight cluster. These overnight clusters are called roosts. Scientists don't know much about these roosts. For instance, how do monarchs choose where to form their roosts? Do the same monarch butterflies always roost together?

The locations of roosts can provide important information about the routes, or "flyways," that the monarchs take on their way to the Mexican overwintering sites. Remember from Chapter Two that Dr. Fred and Norah Urquhart used recaptured tagged monarchs to figure out where the butterflies were going in the fall. If you connect the dots between where a monarch was tagged and where it was seen again, you get a straight line. However, surely monarch butterflies don't fly in a straight line down to Mexico. Roost sighting data from Journey North might provide a more accurate sense of the flyways that monarch butterflies take on their long fall migration.

In 2005, Journey North put out a call online asking people to record when and where they saw a monarch butterfly roost in the fall, which could be in the evening or the early morning. To qualify as a roost, there had to be at least twelve butterflies in the cluster. Roost

**FIGURE 6-4.** Photos of monarch butterfly roosts submitted to Journey North. (A) Enid, OK. (B) Watertown, SD. (C) Texas City, TX. (D) Bolivar, TX.

sightings were collected each year starting in the third week of August through to the end of October. (Journey North still collects roost sightings to this day. If you are lucky enough to see one, be sure to enter your sighting at the Journey North website!)

Within the first three years of their call-out to the public, Journey North received over 600 roost sightings. Each sighting was placed as a dot on a map at the location where the sighting was reported. When all the sightings

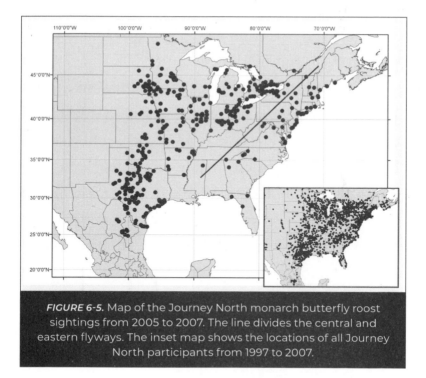

**FIGURE 6-5.** Map of the Journey North monarch butterfly roost sightings from 2005 to 2007. The line divides the central and eastern flyways. The inset map shows the locations of all Journey North participants from 1997 to 2007.

were placed on the map, Howard and Dr. Davis saw there were two separate groups taking two separate flyways. One flyway, with the largest group, went through the center of the monarch breeding range. Howard and Dr. Davis called this the central flyway. There was also a second, less populated flyway that went along the northeast, mid-Atlantic, and coastal plain states, and appeared to stop near the Carolinas. Howard and Dr. Davis named this the eastern flyway. They also noticed that no roosts were spotted in the states of Alabama, Louisiana, and Mississippi, even though many Journey North participants lived there.

Roost sighting data provides important details about the routes the butterflies travel in the fall to reach Mexico. As Howard and Dr. Davis point out in their report, seeing these details allows people to work toward preserving habitat in those areas. Specifically, the butterflies need trees and bushes to rest on, and enough wildflowers to fuel their bodies for their travels and store fat for the winter.

Howard and Dr. Davis published their findings in the early 2000s. More recently, a team led by Dr. James L. Tracy used newer, more powerful math to analyze the Journey North roosting data.[11] They also included information about potential human-made threats to the monarch migration. They discovered that the central flyway tended to shift as much as 124 miles in some years, especially to the west. They're not sure why. We should keep this in mind when planning habitat conservation efforts for the monarch fall migration.

The two flyways also faced different challenges. Within the central flyway, the team found reports of higher numbers of monarchs being hit by vehicles on roadways. The central flyway also included areas where chemicals are used to protect food crops. The eastern flyway included areas where mosquito-killing chemicals were being sprayed. In their study, the team suggests that perhaps wildflowers could be planted away from roads so that monarchs don't end up being hit by moving cars or being sprayed by trucks filled with anti-mosquito chemicals. However, is there a way to protect these wildflowers from being exposed to the chemicals that are sprayed on the crops? A lot more work needs to

---

11. Not only do scientists make scientific discoveries, but mathematicians make mathematical discoveries, too. Mathematicians can develop new techniques that allow scientists to perform new and more powerful analyses on their data. Just like how our knowledge of science evolves, so does our knowledge of math.

be done to ensure that the monarchs' migratory flyways are safe and provide all the resources the monarchs need.

Scientists continue to explore Journey North's data to this day. Journey North wouldn't be possible without the involvement of everyday people like you and me. "The connection between scientists and the community of observers has been really rich," Howard said. "Just people out looking. People out looking and observing things that scientists could never have the eyes and ears to. Or time. Or money. It's all been super powerful in terms of education and good science." One thing Howard said that Dr. Brower told her over and over again was "Without this sort of citizen input, imagine how much we would never know!"

Monarch Watch and Journey North both focus on tracking adult monarch butterflies as they travel across the continent. Are there other ways we can keep tabs on monarch butterflies and learn more about monarch science and conservation? Let's dive into the next chapter and see.

## CHAPTER SEVEN

# TRACKING MORE THAN MIGRATION

Dr. Karen Oberhauser had been curious about monarch butterflies since she was a kid. She started studying them in earnest when she was a graduate student in the 1980s. Later, she inherited eighty acres of farmland in western Wisconsin from her grandfather. That's almost the size of eighty football fields. The land was grassy, speckled with wildflower patches here and there, and milkweed dotted the landscape, too. It was the perfect setting to continue her research. However, by this time, Dr. Oberhauser was not so much interested in the adult butterflies fluttering around, but rather the monarch eggs and **larvae** (caterpillars) that she hoped to find clinging to the milkweed. She knew people tracked and counted adult monarch butterflies when the butterflies migrated to and from Mexico, and they measured the size of the overwintering colonies, but no one had measured the population of monarchs in their breeding grounds. Could counting eggs and larvae in spring and summer be an additional way to keep tabs on the status of monarch butterflies?

The farmland Dr. Oberhauser inherited was just one of many monarch butterfly breeding sites across a few states and southern Canada. Dr. Oberhauser had a team of only several students. There was no way they could count eggs and larvae across all breeding sites themselves.

Then a new student joined Dr. Oberhauser's team. Her name was Michelle Prysby, and she had an interest in education and outreach. Together, Prysby and Dr. Oberhauser came up with an idea: What if they asked members of the public across the United States and Canada to help count monarch eggs and larvae that they found on milkweed plants? Their idea became the Monarch Larva Monitoring Project.

## THE MONARCH LARVA MONITORING PROJECT

The Monarch Larva Monitoring Project, or the MLMP, was created in 1997. To recruit volunteers, the MLMP team used email distribution lists that already existed for organizations like Monarch Watch. Prysby and other MLMP team members traveled to various nature centers across the United States to hold in-person training sessions about how to find and identify monarch eggs and larvae.

After volunteers searched for eggs and larvae on their own and filled out their data sheets, they mailed them to the MLMP headquarters, which was at the University of Minnesota. The data was entered by hand into a database. It took days between when volunteers mailed their data to when it was entered in the MLMP system. It also required quite a lot of paper and postage stamps.

Today, things are a lot faster and smoother. The MLMP uses social media to attract new volunteers and keep in touch with existing ones, and training can be done virtually. After volunteers collect data, they can submit it online, where it is immediately added to the database, and the data can be seen in real time. The MLMP is now led by Monarch Joint Venture and the University of Wisconsin–Madison Arboretum.

So far, thousands of volunteers across the eastern United States and southern Canada have provided data to the program.

Prysby and Dr. Oberhauser were impressed with the dedication of their volunteers. "The most surprising and rewarding parts of the project stem from the incredible dedication of our volunteers," said Dr. Oberhauser, "and how seriously they take their 'job' of providing quality data that help us understand monarchs."

Prysby agreed. "People's passion for monarchs was surprising to me, and how excited people were to do anything related to monarchs. There are other citizen science projects out there where you just collect one piece of data and you're done. This one can be more demanding. But people are still interested and want to make a difference."

By 2014, evidence showed that the area monarch butterflies occupy at the Mexican overwintering sites was getting smaller and smaller. This suggested that the number of monarch butterflies in eastern North America was dropping. Was the number of monarch butterfly eggs and surviving larvae in eastern North America shrinking, too? By then the MLMP database had seventeen years' worth of data. Dr. Oberhauser decided to dig into it. She and her team discovered that monarchs tend to lay more eggs in very small habitats quite spread out from one another, such as backyard gardens, compared to other sites, such as prairies, cropland, and state parks. This shows that monarch butterflies are excellent at searching huge areas and finding pockets of milkweed in fields, small towns, suburban areas, and cities. It's quite impressive when you think about it, that a tiny butterfly can find a particular type of plant among so many distractions in the world, especially when they are able to find only one or two plants that happen to be in a city garden, or one or two plants that managed to grow in a cornfield. "We would find monarch eggs and caterpillars on milkweed in the middle of a cornfield where the corn was way, way higher than the milkweed," recalled Prysby. "Monarchs were flying into the cornfields and using the milkweed there. We were pretty surprised by that." How monarchs detect milkweed is a mystery waiting to be solved.

It is important to realize that monarch butterflies have always been good at finding milkweed, but over the past few decades, they've had to sharpen their skills.

Vast expanses of land that used to host wild plants like milkweed have been converted to monocultures of corn, soybeans, and other crops. Land has also been turned into cities. Habitat loss has forced monarch butterflies to be better milkweed detectives.

The MLMP data also showed that the number of monarch eggs per milkweed plant (or egg density) across the United States and southern Canada varied greatly from year to year. Some years the MLMP volunteers found lots of eggs, and other years they found fewer. Weather was probably one reason for this. But overall, monarch egg densities have been declining since 2006. Dr. Oberhauser and her team found that lower densities of monarch butterfly eggs and more land being taken over by crops predicts a smaller number of monarchs that make it to Mexico in the winter. This leads to a shrinking population of monarch butterflies. However, these findings can be used to encourage people to create monarch habitats. Unlike many other animals threatened with extinction, monarch butterflies can use a variety of different habitats—cities, suburbs, prairies, and farmers' fields, to name a few—as long as they provide milkweed and nectar flowers and are free of pesticides. Before **herbicide-resistant crops** came along, monarchs used to thrive in crops such as corn. Can we start devoting some cropland to milkweed and other wild native plants? Even better, can we rethink and revise agricultural policies so that they no longer encourage large swaths of land to be changed and used as crop monocultures?

As we've seen, data gathered through citizen science suggests we should provide monarch butterflies with more milkweed. Is there a way to plant milkweed that will most benefit the monarchs? For instance, should we plant milkweed in patches or should it be spread out? If in patches, how big should the patches be? Should it be in the middle of fields or on the outskirts? We will now meet a young scientist who is interested in these questions and is trying to answer them by tracking the movements of individual monarch butterflies.

## CORNFIELDS AND TINY TRANSMITTERS
Dr. Kelsey Fisher has loved science ever since she was little. In college she majored in biology and joined a research group one summer that studied native butterflies and their host plants. She found it super interesting, so she stayed with the project while she completed her degree. By the time she graduated, she knew she wanted

to study insects. For her master's degree at the University of Delaware, she focused on the plant preferences of the European corn borer. Then she heard of a group of researchers at Iowa State University who study monarch butterflies. It was an opportunity she felt she couldn't pass up. "There are people all over the university working together on monarch butterflies from different perspectives," said Dr. Fisher. "It's a really big team. There are people studying **agronomy, entomology**, weed science, natural resource ecology and management, and evolutionary ecology. We're trying to tie it all together so that we can have a pretty sound conservation strategy for the state of Iowa." Dr. Fisher was hooked. She applied and was accepted to the doctoral program.

For her PhD research, Dr. Fisher decided to study movement ecology of monarch butterflies. "My research is trying to figure out where to put the milkweed," Dr. Fisher explained. "We need the monarchs to be able to find it and interact with it. The more time the monarchs spend with milkweed, that's more eggs. And then that's more caterpillars, more butterflies, and ultimately a larger overwintering population."

As Dr. Fisher explained, if female monarch butterflies find a patch of milkweed, they don't tend to stay there. They leave and go somewhere else, dispersing their eggs across a wide area. "We want the female monarchs to be able to find another patch of milkweed really easily," said Dr. Fisher. "Because if they can't find it, then they will waste a lot of time and energy wandering, trying to find more milkweed. I'm looking to see what decisions they make. Are they influenced by wind direction? How far can they see and smell milkweed? If they leave a patch and there's another one down the block, do they know it's there, and how long does it take them to get there? How long do they spend in a habitat before they leave it?"

Dr. Fisher read about how scientists tracked other, bigger animals, like birds and wolves, using a method called **radio telemetry**. Radio telemetry has three parts. First, there is a **radio transmitter**. This is a device that the animal wears, and it sends out an invisible radio signal. For big animals like wolves, the radio transmitter can be attached to a collar that the animal wears around its neck. For small birds, the transmitter is strapped onto their lower back.

Next, the scientist holds a **radio antenna** that picks up the signals that are sent from the radio transmitter. Finally, a **radio receiver** turns the signals into beeps. As the animal gets closer, the beeps become louder. This way, the scientist can get a good idea about where the animal is without having to actually chase it and keep an eye on it.

Dr. Fisher thought that radio telemetry would be a cool way to track monarchs, but are there radio transmitters small enough for butterflies? Thanks to advances in technology, there are now radio transmitters that are small enough to fit on insects. Dr. Fisher found radio transmitters that are smaller than a sunflower seed, weighing 220 milligrams. Monarch butterflies weigh about 500 milligrams, less than a dollar bill. To make sure the radio transmitters would not be too heavy for the butterflies to wear, she did a test with watch batteries. Watch batteries weigh a bit more than the radio transmitters and are much less expensive. (Each radio transmitter costs $200.) If monarch butterflies could wear a watch battery and fly and behave normally, then they could certainly wear a radio transmitter.

Dr. Fisher and her team of students caught wild monarch butterflies and superglued watch batteries to

FIGURE 7-1. A monarch butterfly wearing a radio transmitter on the underside of its abdomen (top) and a monarch butterfly wearing a watch battery on the underside of its abdomen (bottom).

their abdomens. Then they put the butterfly to sleep on dry ice before releasing it. If they released the butterfly right away, it would panic and fly straight up into the air. It was then impossible to see any of the butterfly's natural behavior. (Wouldn't you panic, too, if a giant grabbed you and stuck a strange metal object to your belly?) Dr. Fisher used dry ice because it's frozen carbon dioxide, so as it melts, it releases carbon dioxide and puts the butterfly to sleep. Also, dry ice is colder than ice made from water, and coldness puts insects to sleep. Finally, dry ice doesn't make a mess when it melts, unlike water ice.

When the butterflies were taken off the dry ice, they woke up and flew, drank nectar from flowers, and rested normally. The watch batteries could be removed from the butterfly by gently peeling them off. The butterflies were not harmed at all. Assured that the radio transmitters would not affect the monarch butterflies' natural behavior, Dr. Fisher could start her experiment—the first time that radio telemetry would be used with monarchs.

Dr. Fisher needed a location to do her research. She found an expanse of restored prairie in Boone, Iowa.

There were grasses, wildflowers here and there, and patches of milkweed. In the distance, tall stalks of corn made an abrupt green wall between natural land and human-made crops. Another side of the prairie met up with a lush, green forest. On yet another side were houses. From Dr. Fisher's point of view, this location was perfect because the monarchs had lots of options for choosing where to fly: prairie, crops, forest, and residential areas. It also represented the Midwest in general, which can be quite fragmented with different land types.

Ready to start the experiment, Dr. Fisher and her team drove to the site in Boone. They parked and pulled all of their equipment out of the trunk. The early-morning August sun was already hot. *No wind. Perfect,* she thought. No wind meant the monarchs could choose where to fly rather than the wind choosing for them. Monarchs are no match for wind gusts.

Dr. Fisher took a nylon mesh cage out of her car. "Hello, you two," she said to the monarchs inside it. Their wings were folded closed as they clasped on to the cage sides.

The research team marched off through the tall

prairie grass. There was Brooklyn, Kevin, Sammi, and Riley—all students working with Dr. Fisher as a summer job and eager to get experience with scientific fieldwork. Each student held an antenna, a handheld radio receiver, and a compass. As their voices drifted farther away, Dr. Fisher could hear them discussing which corner of the prairie each person would take. With monarchs and equipment in tow, Dr. Fisher headed for the center of the field.

After choosing a spot, Dr. Fisher bent down and placed her equipment and the mesh cage on the ground. She stood up and shielded her eyes from the bright sun. In the distance she could see each of her teammates in separate corners of the field. Seconds later, they all checked in with their walkie-talkies.

*Ready!*

*All set!*

*Good to go!*

*Let's do this!*

Dr. Fisher reached into the mesh cage and plucked out one of the monarch butterflies, gently holding the wings between her first and middle fingers. Despite the many times she had held monarchs this way, she was always amazed at how the wings felt like nothing, delicate and less than paper thin. "It's okay, little one. I've got you," she whispered. She attached one of the tiny radio transmitters onto the monarch's abdomen: drop of glue, press, hold, place her on dry ice. After waiting a few heartbeats, she removed the monarch from the dry ice and cupped her in her hands. The monarch lay still. Then her legs wiggled, her proboscis uncurled and curled back up, and her wings opened and closed a few times. As the monarch stood up, Dr. Fisher felt the tickle of her feet on her palm. The monarch flapped her wings several times and then in a blink, she took off. Dr. Fisher watched as the butterfly fluttered here and there, as if getting her bearings, and then she flew in a more direct course farther away. "Show us your stuff, lovely girl," Dr. Fisher whispered.

The monarch looked like a small flickering speck, but Dr. Fisher could still see her. The monarch landed on a patch of wildflowers, rested (maybe drank some nectar? Dr. Fisher couldn't tell), and then flittered to another patch. The butterfly stayed within the prairie for quite a while, seeming to zig and zag this way and that between flowers. Dr. Fisher knew that her four teammates, who were each at a corner of the prairie, would be hearing beeps coming from their handheld receivers. The beeping would get louder the closer the monarch flew to them. Every minute they would record the compass bearing of the beeps. Later, back at the lab, they would use a special computer program that would analyze all the compass bearings from the beeps, to reconstruct the flight path of the butterfly.

Dr. Fisher glanced at her watch. Thirty minutes had passed since she released the monarch. Nine more minutes and they'd reach their cutoff time when they would try to recapture her. She continued to watch the monarch, which was now a tiny dot in the distance. Suddenly, the butterfly zipped up and over the wall of cornstalks on the far side of the prairie. She disappeared into the cornfield! Dr. Fisher snatched her butterfly net off the ground and raced toward the corn. Kevin, who was standing closest to where the monarch disappeared, dove into the cornstalks. Hopefully, the beeps from his handheld receiver would help find the monarch. Soon Dr. Fisher was pushing her way through the cornstalks beside him. As they made their way through the tall, green, leafy plants, Kevin held the antenna up high, hoping to catch a signal.

"I don't see her," said Dr. Fisher as she scanned the sky above the corn.

"Neither do I," said Kevin.

*Beep . . . beep . . . BEEP!*

"She's close," said Dr. Fisher as she gripped her net. "Oh! I see her!"

A few paces ahead, a flicker of orange and black floated above the cornstalks. Dr. Fisher ran after her and raised her net high into the air. She aimed and *SWISH!* She missed. She stumbled but regained her balance.

Dr. Fisher and Kevin continued to crash through the cornstalks, trying not to lose each other. The receiver stopped beeping. Dr. Fisher thought of the expensive little radio transmitter attached to the butterfly. *Great,* she thought. *There goes two hundred dollars down the drain.* She owned several transmitters, but she was hoping that whenever she could, she could gently peel off the transmitter from one monarch and use it for another, rather than letting her equipment flutter away in the breeze.

*BEEP!*

"There she is!" Kevin pointed above their heads.

Dr. Fisher raised her net and *SWISH!* She got her!

"Yes!" Dr. Fisher and Kevin cheered.

Dr. Fisher spun the net handle in her hand so that the mesh folded over itself, trapping the monarch at the tip of the netting. She gripped the netting with her other hand partway down so the butterfly couldn't escape. Dr. Fisher and Kevin picked their way back through the cornstalks to the open prairie, where they would have more room to remove the transmitter and set the butterfly free.

After gluing the transmitter onto the second monarch from the mesh cage, Dr. Fisher and her team watched as it, too, fluttered from flower patch to flower patch in the open prairie. This one was much easier to catch after the thirty-nine-minute cutoff time, as it had zipped to the outskirts of a surrounding forest and landed on the side of a tree. The team caught two more wild monarchs and tested them, too. They also caught three monarchs they would keep overnight in the mesh cage to test the next morning. Until they were tested, the captured butterflies could feast on fruit punch Gatorade.

By the end of the summer, the team had tested a total of thirteen monarch butterflies. There was enough data to do some analyses. Dr. Fisher used a special computer program to look for patterns in all the information from the radio transmitters. Did the flight paths of the butterflies share something in common? She hoped so. She studied the numbers and diagrams on her computer screen, and then suddenly felt an inward burst of excitement. There was a pattern! In the prairie, the monarchs tended to take between two and thirty small "steps" while turning around often. These steps were about 160 feet or less. Most of the time, the butterflies were feeding from patches of prairie wildflowers. They would turn around a lot, probably in order to stay within a patch and feed from as many blossoms as possible. Then suddenly, *BAM!* The butterfly left the prairie and flew straight into the surrounding forest, cornfield, or road. Dr. Fisher said it was as if the monarchs eventually had enough of the patches of flowers in the prairie and said, "I'm outta here!"

It's really cool that Dr. Fisher discovered that the monarchs tended to take a bunch of little hops among the flowers, then a huge step out of the field. But what she was really happy about was that her method of using radio telemetry with monarch butterflies worked. "We knew that monarchs move like crazy, but nobody has been able to explore that," she said. "Up until now, once the butterfly leaves a patch, we've just been like, 'It flew in that direction.' Now we can follow it. This is big!"

With technology advancing all the time, it is becoming easier to track monarch butterflies in greater detail, whether they are flying all the way to Mexico, flying northward with the spring, or fluttering from flower patch to flower patch. But how do the butterflies know where to go? How do they make it to the Mexican over-wintering sites when they have never been there before? And how do they know where to go when it's spring-time? What goes on in their little heads? We'll explore that next.

## CHAPTER EIGHT

# MONARCH "SMARTS"

The monarch butterfly migration is incredible, and it's a marvel it can happen in the first place. Think about it: Each fall, monarch butterflies, which are spread out over millions of square miles across southern Canada and the northern United States, fly about 3,000 miles south, then gather in an area that is approximately 73 miles wide. They do this with a brain that's the size of a pinhead. What's more, they've never been to Mexico before. No one has taught them where to go. They just "know." How do they know where to fly?

I am particularly excited about this question because it ventures into the field that I studied in school and that I am passionate about: **animal cognition**. This is the area of science that explores how nonhuman animals think, learn, remember, and make decisions. Wouldn't it be extraordinary to peek inside the brain of a migrating monarch butterfly as it flies to the Trans-Mexican Volcanic Belt and figure out how they accomplish such a feat? Many scientists have attempted to do so. Well, not all of them actually looked at monarch brains. Instead, they designed some clever experiments to gather clues about how it is that such a seemingly delicate, small-brained butterfly can navigate successfully across a continent.

### STRAWS, COMPUTER BITS, AND BEESWAX

How do you even begin to figure out how monarch butterflies migrate? Scientists tried to imagine what you need to know to be able to travel somewhere. You need to know what direction to go in and you need something to guide you in that direction. Maybe there's something in the environment that monarchs use as a kind of compass. Monarchs fly only during the daytime, so the most obvious and reliable cue they could follow to help them travel in a certain direction is the sun. One problem with using the sun to navigate is that it moves across the sky as the day progresses. As the sun moves, so would the direction you're traveling in. You would not end up flying in a straight line. Do monarchs have some kind of way to internally compensate for the time of day? Can their brains do that? How can we find out?

To see whether monarch butterflies have a "time-compensated sun compass," Dr. Henrik Mouritsen and Dr. Barrie J. Frost built a flight simulator for monarchs. They built it out of a large, white, translucent plastic cylinder, twenty-five inches high and twenty-three inches in diameter. A rod was placed across the top of the cylinder, and a butterfly was attached with beeswax to a little shaft in the middle (see Figure 8-1). To allow the butterfly to turn in any direction it wanted, they created a tiny contraption using a plastic axle from a computer mouse. (Pretty clever, if you ask me.) The butterfly couldn't fly anywhere since it was stuck in place, but it could freely flap its wings and turn in any direction as though it were flying. A computer recorded the direction the butterfly "flew" in, and there were mini cameras to let the scientists watch the butterfly from outside the cylinder. To encourage the attached butterfly to "fly," Dr. Mouritsen

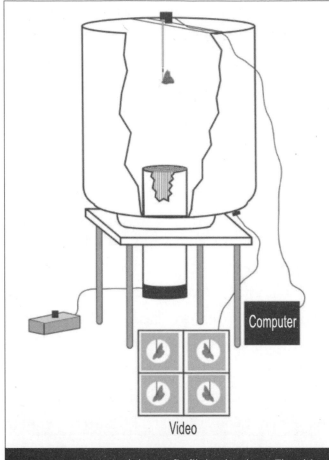

**FIGURE 8-1.** A monarch butterfly flight simulator. The side is cut away so we can see the butterfly attached to the shaft hanging from the top. Attached to the shaft is a computer that keeps track of the direction the butterfly "flies" in. Small cameras on the bottom of the cylinder let the scientists watch the butterfly from outside the simulator. The pipe through the middle of the simulator blows a steady stream of air to encourage the butterfly to fly. The pipe is cut away so we can see the hundreds of drinking straws that help create a gentle, straight breeze.

and Dr. Frost hooked up a fan to the bottom of the cylinder that carefully blew air through hundreds of parallel drinking straws so the breeze was gentle and straight. (Again, quite clever.) When the fan blew air, the monarch butterfly attached to the shaft would begin flapping its wings and start to fly. The scientists could then measure the direction the butterfly was flying in.

After building their flight simulator, Dr. Mouritsen and Dr. Frost collected monarch butterflies that were roosting nearby on the shore of Lake Ontario. Due to the time of year and the butterflies' roosting behavior, the scientists were certain these monarchs were ready to migrate to Mexico. They kept the butterflies inside for five days. During this time, they divided the butterflies into three groups. They made each group adjust to a different "time zone." For the first group, over the five days the scientists turned the lights on and off at around the same time that the sun naturally rises and sets at that time of year: The lights came on around 7:00 a.m. and shut off at around 7:00 p.m. For the second group, the scientists always turned the lights on at 1:00 a.m. and off at 1:00 p.m. For these butterflies, the sunrise and sunset times were advanced by six hours. For the third group, the lights always came on at 1:00 p.m. and off at 1:00 a.m. These butterflies were "delayed" by six hours. After five days, all three groups of butterflies had adjusted to their new time zones, and it was time to put them in the flight simulator.

The scientists placed the flight simulator outside in the sunshine and attached the butterflies to the simulator one at a time. They turned on the fan. Each butterfly flapped its wings really fast as if it was actually flying. Most butterflies flew steadily in the simulator for at least an hour (that's a long time, when you think about it), and some monarchs flew for as long as four hours! In many instances, the scientists had to stop the butterfly so that another one could have a turn. Interestingly, when they gently turned the shaft that the butterfly was attached to, which changed the direction in which the butterfly was flying, the butterfly slowly shifted its direction back to the original direction in which it was going. The whole time, the computer attached to the flight simulator recorded the direction in which the monarch was pointing. When the butterflies were done with the test, the scientists freed them by gently melting the beeswax and then releasing the butterfly back into the wild.

What did the scientists find? Butterflies that did not have their time zone shifted flew in the expected direction if they were migrating normally to Mexico. However, butterflies that had their sunrise and sunset times shifted flew in different directions. They thought it was a different time of day, so they compensated their flight direction when they saw the sun. This is evidence that monarch butterflies use a time-compensated sun compass to migrate to Mexico.

Monarch butterflies also use their time-compensated sun compass when migrating north in spring. How do they know to fly north? The cold weather at the Mexican overwintering sites has something to do with it. Dr. Steven M. Reppert and his team at the University of Massachusetts Chan Medical School found that when monarch butterflies are exposed to cold temperatures for several weeks—the kind of temperatures they experience at the Mexican overwintering grounds— their flight direction is recalibrated so that they fly north rather than south or southwest. Monarchs that did not experience coldness continued to orient southward. Something about the cold helps to flick a switch inside monarch butterflies to make them fly in a different direction when it is spring.

The next question was: Where is this compass and how does it work? After all, scientists are curious. They want to take stuff apart to figure out exactly how something operates. The most obvious place to start looking for the time-compensated sun compass is in the monarch butterfly's brain.

Scientists knew that sunlight used for guiding direction first has to be detected by the monarch's eye. Cells in the monarch's eye then carry this information to a bunch of neurons (brain cells) called the **central complex** in the monarch's brain. The central complex is likely where the monarch's compass is found. Around the early 2000s, reports were being published that other insects such as flies and moths have clocklike systems that trigger them to eat and mate. These "clocks" were not in their brain but in other body areas, like their antennae. Perhaps the monarch butterfly clock is not in their brain but in their antennae. To test this, Dr. Reppert and his team decided to surgically remove the antennae of a group of monarch butterflies (poor monarchs!). Next, the butterflies were made to adjust to different time zones as in the experiment described earlier, and then were placed in the flight simulator. The monarchs flew just as strongly and consistently as the monarchs who had antennae, but they flew in random directions. This shows that monarchs need their antennae to fly in the correct direction to get to Mexico and to fly back north in the spring.

The next question was: Do the antennae of monarch butterflies actually detect sunlight? The scientists did something very simple and clever (although likely not comfortable for the monarchs): Before they attached the butterflies one at a time to the flight simulator, they painted the antennae of some of the butterflies black, and they painted the antennae of other butterflies with a clear, see-through paint that allowed light to pass through it. Butterflies that had clear paint on their antennae flew in the direction we would expect them to fly if they were migrating to Mexico. Butterflies with black paint on their antennae flew in all sorts of directions. (Some butterflies would probably have ended up in Alaska if they weren't attached to the simulator.) Butterflies thus need their antennae to navigate. Specifically, their antennae need light from the sun to synchronize their antennal clocks to the current sunrise and sunset times. Their antennae, therefore, provide the timing component of the time-compensated sun compass system.

This discovery was extremely exciting. Antennae were always thought to allow insects to smell. And they do, and this is an important function, but now scientists are gradually discovering that antennae have additional roles, like acting as a time-compensated sun compass. For some insects, antennae can also detect gravity, wind, and sound. Think about how thin and delicate antennae are. That's a lot to pack into such small, slender structures. Who knew antennae could be so complex? And there are more questions to explore. Do the antennae act completely alone to provide the monarch butterfly with timing information? Or do they work with the butterfly's brain? When it comes time for the antennae to send information to the brain to influence the butterfly's behavior (that is, to decide in which direction to fly), where is this "circuit" that connects the antennae and the brain, and how does it work? Do other insects like ants, bees, and locusts also have a time-compensated sun compass in their antennae? Or are monarch butterflies unique in this way?

Monarch butterflies have been seen flying in the right direction, toward Mexico, on overcast days. Somehow, they are able to navigate without the sun. To find out how they do this, scientists looked to other animals that migrate, such as birds and sea turtles. One cue these animals use to make sure they are traveling in the right direction is the earth's magnetic field. As shown in Figure 8-2, the earth has a magnetic field,

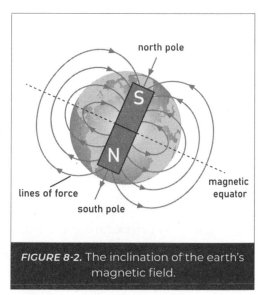

FIGURE 8-2. The inclination of the earth's magnetic field.

and the angle of this magnetic field changes as you move north or south.

Animals like birds and sea turtles are able to detect changes in the angle of the magnetic field as they move, and they use this information to travel in the correct direction for their migration. Unlike the sun, which moves throughout the day, the earth's magnetic fields are fixed. Therefore, an animal's inner magnetic compass does not need time compensation.

Do monarch butterflies use a magnetic compass, too? Dr. Reppert and his team placed a special coil around their flight simulator that allowed them to adjust the magnetic field that the monarch butterflies experienced inside. From other experiments with flies, birds, and lizards, they knew that the ability of animals to sense the earth's magnetic field seems to depend on their also detecting a certain wavelength of light that is invisible to humans: ultraviolet (UV)A/blue light. Perhaps monarchs are the same way. So, the team shone UVA/blue light into the simulator. Sure enough, monarch butterflies that were placed in the simulator adjusted their flight direction depending on the magnetic field in the simulator, showing that monarchs can navigate using a magnetic compass.

Where is this magnetic compass in monarch butterflies? Dr. Reppert and his team suspected it's in the antennae. Once again, for some monarch butterflies they painted their antennae black, and for others they painted their antennae with clear paint. Butterflies with black paint on their antennae no longer flew in predictable directions. Once more, the antennae seem to be the sweet spot for monarch butterfly navigation. (Those amazing antennae!) So, like other migrating animals, such as birds and sea turtles, monarch butterflies can detect the earth's magnetic field and use it on overcast days.[12]

12. To learn more about Dr. Reppert's cool and important research, visit reppertlab.org.

Interestingly, back in the 1980s, Fernando Ortíz Monasterio and other members of Pro Monarca suspected that monarch butterflies use the earth's magnetic field to migrate to their overwintering sites each year. They pointed out that monarchs contain a naturally occurring magnetic mineral called **magnetite**, and that the overwintering sites are located in an area with particularly strong magnetic fields. Research by Dr. Reppert and other scientists suggest that Pro Monarca's suspicions were correct.

While migrating, monarchs often have to deal with a significant challenge: They can easily be shoved off course by a gust of wind. How do they get back on course after being blown around? The monarchs' antennae have sensors that can detect changes in wind direction and can help them get back on track. But there are other helpful cues. For instance, as they reach Texas, the Gulf of Mexico will be on the left and the Rocky Mountains (and eventually the Sierra Madre Occidental) will be on their right. Do the monarchs see these huge landmarks and use them to navigate to the right place? Or do the oyamel fir trees in the Mexican mountains give off a certain scent? Butterflies are very good at detecting smells. Another possibility is the presence of other monarchs.

After all, as we've learned, large groups of monarchs roost in trees overnight on their way to Mexico, and monarchs can often be seen flying together. Do monarch butterflies use some kind of "follow-the-leader" strategy? Butterflies are especially good when it comes to detecting **pheromones** (special chemicals) given off by other butterflies, so maybe that plays a role in it. There are a lot of questions that remain to be answered about the great eastern monarch butterfly migration.

## MILKWEED DETECTIVES

As we saw in Chapter Seven, despite the complexity of the world around us, monarch butterflies are able to find milkweed plants on which to lay their eggs. There are all different kinds of milkweeds that flower in a variety of colors. When milkweed plants are in bloom, they are pretty easy to spot, but when monarchs start making their way north from Mexico in March, milkweed is often just green and leafy. Green like the grasses and leaves of other plants that probably surround it. How are monarch butterflies able to find the milkweed? Do they know the particular shape of milkweed leaves? Is the green of milkweed leaves somehow distinct from other greens?

That's assuming monarch butterflies are mainly

guided by sight. This is a very humanlike way to think about the world. Most humans rely a lot on vision. But that's not necessarily the case for other animals. Two scientists, Dr. Tom Eisner and Dr. Jerry Meinwald, once wrote, "Ours is a world of sights and sounds. We live by our eyes and ears and tend generally to be oblivious to the chemical happenings in our surrounds." Monarch butterflies have a number of different **chemoreceptors** on their bodies. Chemoreceptors are structures that detect chemicals in the environment. They come in different shapes and sizes. Certain chemicals fit in chemoreceptors like a key fits in a lock. When that happens, the brain can identify the chemical. We have chemoreceptors on our tongue—our taste buds—that enable us to sense taste. Our nose is also filled with chemoreceptors that enable us to detect smells.

It is possible that monarch butterflies find milkweed plants by both sight and smell. Their antennae might pick up chemical cues from the milkweed that help to guide them closer to the plant, and then, once in range, their eyes can tell them where to land. Scientists aren't sure exactly how the process works. They have watched monarch butterflies flying freely in fields to try to figure out how they choose milkweed plants. Monarchs often fly over many milkweed plants without showing any interest, but then they'll pick a milkweed plant here and there to land on. What is special about these particular plants?

Scientists who watched monarch butterflies in the field collected all the milkweed leaves that the butterflies landed on. They discovered the monarchs were like Goldilocks in a way: They avoided milkweed plants with a cardenolide content that was too high, they avoided plants with a cardenolide content that was too low, but they chose plants with a cardenolide content that was just right. Choosing milkweed plants with a cardenolide content in the midrange makes sense. Milkweed plants with too high a cardenolide content could end up poisoning the caterpillars when the caterpillars eat the leaves, whereas milkweed plants with low cardenolide content will not provide enough poisons for the caterpillars to store in their bodies to protect them from predators. How do monarchs identify milkweed plants with medium levels of cardenolides?

Scientists might not have figured out yet how monarch butterflies choose milkweed plants while in flight, but Dr. Meena Haribal observed that once female monarch butterflies land on milkweed, they often show a variety of interesting behaviors. One cool behavior that she saw—and one you might see, too, if you're lucky enough to spot a female butterfly on a milkweed leaf and look closely—is "drumming." The butterfly will extend her front legs (which are very short) and tap or drum on the leaf really fast. She might drum with her middle legs, too. They do this so fast that it's rather hard to see.

Besides drumming, female monarchs might drag their middle legs across the surface of the milkweed leaf. Their legs have sharp claws on them, so this behavior scratches the leaf's surface. If the plant is a type of milkweed that contains a lot of latex, latex then oozes out from the scratched area. Remember from Chapter One that latex is a white, sticky liquid. It turns clear while it quickly dries. If the milkweed plant doesn't contain much latex, it's hard to see the scratches the monarch makes.

Female monarchs also use their antennae to investigate milkweed leaves. They usually tap the leaf with their antennae's club-shaped end. Dr. Haribal saw that sometimes butterflies tap with only one antenna, and sometimes they use their middle legs to hold down an antenna so that the tip of the antenna touches the leaf for a few seconds. While standing still and holding down an antenna, the monarch might also drag it across the leaf by pulling their middle legs toward them.

Finally, Dr. Haribal saw that sometimes a monarch butterfly might curl her abdomen under the leaf but not touch the leaf. Only when she lays an egg does her abdomen touch the leaf surface. The butterfly might curl and uncurl her abdomen several times while she drums with her legs or taps the leaf with her antennae. Curiously, all these "curlings" do not necessarily lead to egg-laying. It is as if the butterfly is using the tip of her abdomen to test the underside of the leaf for something.

All these curious behaviors Dr. Haribal saw led her to believe that monarch butterflies have chemoreceptors on their feet and antennae. They might also have some kind of receptor at the end of their abdomen, where their **ovipositor** is. (An ovipositor is a special organ insects have that allows them to lay eggs.) She decided to look at these monarch butterfly body parts under a special high-powered microscope, called a **scanning electron microscope**. The images she got are incredible. Not only do they show just how much we humans can't see with our own eyes, but they show that female monarch butterflies' feet and antennae are indeed covered in chemoreceptors, perfect for testing out a milkweed leaf

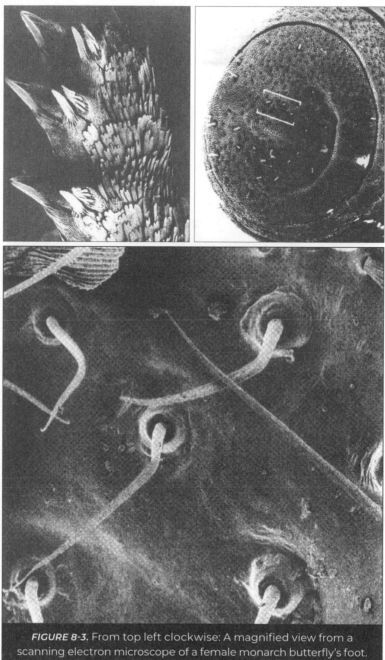

*FIGURE 8-3.* From top left clockwise: A magnified view from a scanning electron microscope of a female monarch butterfly's foot. A magnified view of the tip of a female monarch butterfly's antenna. A magnified view of mechanoreceptors at the end of a female monarch butterfly's abdomen.

when deciding whether or not to lay an egg. The end of a monarch's abdomen seems to be covered in **mechanoreceptors** rather than chemoreceptors. Mechanoreceptors detect touch, pressure, and vibrations.

As if these close-up images weren't amazing enough, when Dr. Haribal looked at her data, she saw that behaviors on milkweed leaves differed from butterfly to butterfly. That is, female monarch butterflies don't use the exact same set of steps to check out a milkweed leaf. The order in which they drum, drag their legs, tap the leaf with their antennae, or curl their abdomen varies, and they might use all these behaviors or just some of them. This suggests that individual monarch butterflies use some kind of decision-making process once they land on a leaf, instead of just using some rigid routine of preprogrammed behaviors. Dr. Haribal suspected that these differences in behavior might be explained by receptor sensitivity, genetics, the butterfly's experience, or even learning. Or maybe a combination of these.

How the butterflies investigated the milkweed leaves in Dr. Haribal's experiment also depended on the type of milkweed plant they landed on. The monarchs seemed to be "investigating" the chemistry of the plant. Dr. Haribal found that milkweed leaves contain chemicals called **flavonoids**, and these flavonoids glow purple under ultraviolet light. Humans can't see the purple glow because we can't see UV light, but monarch butterflies can. Interestingly, scientists have found that some butterflies have eyelike structures on their butts—yes, eyes on their butts!—that can detect UV light. Dr. Haribal wonders if female monarch butterflies use their butts to "see" the chemicals on the surface of the plant—especially the purple flavonoids—when they curl their abdomens under a milkweed leaf. Clearly, a monarch butterfly's decision to lay an egg on a milkweed leaf seems to be a much more complex process than it might appear at first glance.

Monarch butterflies may use their antennae, legs, and butts a lot when checking out milkweed plants, but they still have very large eyes. Vision must still be very important in the life of a monarch butterfly. Do monarchs see color? And if they see color, are they able to learn about different colors in their environment? Let's find out.

### FAVORITE COLORS AND YUCKY NECTAR

When scientists took a close look at monarch butterflies' eyes, they discovered there were three types of cells: one type of cell that can detect UV light, one that can detect blue, and one that can detect green. These cells are very similar to those in bees. However, there was also evidence that some monarch eye cells could filter orange and red.

To discover whether monarch butterflies can tell the difference between colors, Dr. Martha Weiss and her team at Georgetown University set up some very clever but simple experiments. They cut small circles out of colored paper and creased them a little so they had a bit of a flower shape. In the center of each of these "flowers," they stuck a small tube into which the monarch could slip its proboscis. The scientists arranged the flowers in a grid on a large tray of Styrofoam. There were four flowers each of six different colors: red, orange, yellow, blue, purple, and green. The scientists chose these colors because they are spread across the range of colors that monarchs were thought to be able to see. The tray of flowers was then placed inside a mesh cage. To get monarch butterflies interested in visiting the paper flowers, the scientists first gently held each monarch butterfly in their hand and offered them a paper flower like the ones in the mesh cage, only it was made of black paper. In the tube in the center was sugary water to mimic flower nectar. The scientists used a pin to carefully uncurl the butterfly's proboscis and guide it into the nectar tube. This way, the butterfly would learn that they could sip "nectar" from the paper flowers. The team then released the butterfly into the cage with the array of colored paper flowers. Would the butterflies show a preference for certain colors?

It turns out the monarch butterflies' favorite color was orange. They landed on orange flowers more often than on any of the other colors. Purple was their least preferred color, since hardly any butterflies landed on purple flowers. The scientists then repeated the experiment with only three colors: yellow, red, and blue. This time the monarchs' favorite color was yellow. The fact that the monarchs showed a preference for a particular color of flower is evidence that they can see and discriminate between different colors.

Dr. Weiss and her team decided to do one more test. First, they let monarch butterflies drink sugar water from paper flowers that were either red, purple, blue, or yellow. Each butterfly was assigned only one color. Then the monarchs were released one at a time into the mesh cage. In the cage was an array of paper flowers on the Styrofoam tray, but this time the flowers were in various shades of gray, and one flower was the same color as the one the butterfly was trained to drink from. What type of flower would the butterflies land on—the flower that was the same color as their training flower, or one of the gray flowers? The monarchs overwhelmingly chose the colored flower. Since the butterflies could pick out the colored flower among all the grays, this shows that monarch butterflies can detect color.

This gray versus colored flower experiment is cool on another level, because it shows that monarch butterflies are capable of learning. Specifically, it shows that even though they may prefer orange or yellow flowers, they can learn to gather nectar from flowers that are red, purple, or blue. Dr. Weiss and her team did a number of other experiments as well. For instance, after being trained to gather nectar from flowers of one color, monarchs can learn to switch to another color. Monarch butterflies can also learn to gather nectar from flowers of a particular shape (squares or circles), regardless of what color the flowers are. They can learn shape and color combinations, and they can learn to avoid flowers of a certain color that contain salt water (*blech!*) instead of sugar water.

If we try to imagine ourselves as monarch butterflies, the results of these experiments make a lot of sense. Both male and female monarchs need to find flowers so they can drink nectar for energy, and flowers come in all different shapes and colors. Many flowers are yellow, such as goldenrod, which monarchs seem to be attracted to. Especially for monarchs that migrate across North America, it would be handy to be able to learn the different colors and shapes of flowers that offer good nectar. Monarchs will encounter different flowers along their journey, so it's an advantage to be flexible in their flower choices and to be able to learn new flower cues.

It's quite interesting that the monarchs' "favorite" color is orange. Could monarchs have a fondness for orange because that's the color of their wings? Are they attracted to orange so they can find and follow one another, especially during migration and mating? Dr. Weiss and her team aren't sure. Perhaps the ability of monarchs to learn shapes comes in handy when female monarchs are looking for milkweed. Can female monarchs recognize milkweed plants according to the shape of the leaves? Are there other aspects about flowers (and about the environment as a whole), besides color and shape, that monarchs can learn and remember? There are a ton of questions about monarch cognition that science can one day help us answer. Maybe you've thought of some questions yourself.

## CHAPTER NINE

# MONARCHS AROUND THE WORLD

Where did monarch butterflies come from? Did they evolve from some prehistoric ancestor millions of years ago? Imagine huge butterflies the size of kites flapping around during the age of the dinosaurs, since everything back then seems to have been much bigger. Maybe now and then, these prehistoric butterflies landed peacefully on the snout of a T. rex or on the horn of a triceratops. To discover the origins of monarch butterflies, and butterflies more generally, we need to get our hands on some fossils.

## DINOSAURS AND NOSE HAIRS

Piecing together the history of monarch butterflies, and the history of butterflies and moths in general, has been a very tricky business. Fewer fossils of butterflies or butterfly-like insects have been found compared to other types of insects, such as beetles and flies. One reason is because the bodies of butterflies are quite fragile. When a prehistoric butterfly died and was submerged in dirt that would later become rock, its body (or most of it) had a high chance of decomposing and breaking apart, making it very hard for scientists millions of years later to identify what type of insect the body parts belonged to. Dead butterflies might have also been eaten by predators, erasing any evidence that the butterfly existed.

Some prehistoric insects have been preserved in amber, which is fossilized tree resin. **Resin** is secreted by many trees, slowly sliding down the tree's trunk and branches, surrounding and trapping any poor insect that can't escape in time. The resin then hardens and becomes amber. Very few prehistoric butterfly or moth specimens have been found in amber, probably because they could just fly away from an oozy tree. Nonflying insects, like ants, were often not so lucky.

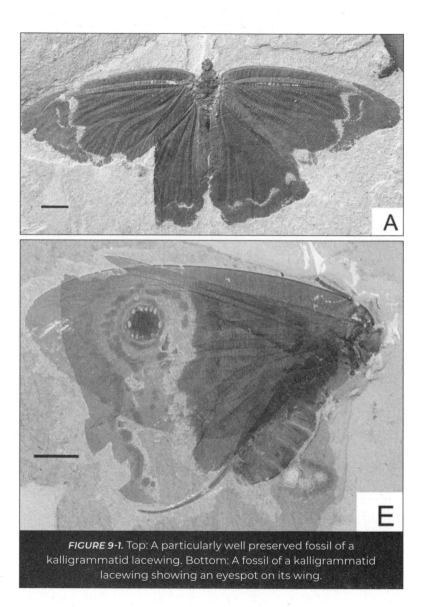

**FIGURE 9-1.** Top: A particularly well preserved fossil of a kalligrammatid lacewing. Bottom: A fossil of a kalligrammatid lacewing showing an eyespot on its wing.

Fortunately, some fossils of butterfly-like insects have been discovered. Scientists call them *Kalligrammatidae*, or **kalligrammatid lacewings**, and sometimes refer to them as the "butterflies of the Jurassic." Some particularly well preserved fossils from China show that they had a wingspan of about six inches (okay, so they weren't as big as kites), and some of the fossils show that their wings had patterns, such as the eyespots that we see on some butterfly wings today.

Fossils of kalligrammatid lacewings are around 165 to 125 million years old. That puts them in the Jurassic and Cretaceous periods, during the era of the dinosaurs. So, maybe prehistoric butterflies *did* land on a T. rex's snout or a triceratops's horn at some point. Or fluttered among a herd of grazing diplodocus. Kalligrammatids were alive about 30 million years before flowering plants, known as **angiosperms**, existed on Earth. This makes the existence of kalligrammatids kind of weird. If there were no flowers to sip nectar from, what did they eat? It turns out that during the age of the dinosaurs, while there were no flowers (that we know of), there were plenty of cone-making plants and trees, called **gymnosperms**. Today's gymnosperms include pine trees, spruce trees, and **cycads** (also known as sago palms), which look like squat palm trees.[13] Kalligrammatids probably ate sugary droplets that oozed from these plants' cones. Some kalligrammatid fossils include what appear to be bits of pollen around or close to the insects' mouthparts, so they likely snacked on pollen produced by gymnosperms as well.

Kalligrammatids were thought to be the closest link to modern butterflies until just a few years ago. A group of scientists drilled deep into the ground in northern Germany in an area that was once an ancient lagoon. They drilled down until they reached sediment that was 200 million years old. This marked the time of a mass extinction event that ended the Triassic period and brought in the Jurassic. The scientists were on the hunt for traces of ancient pollen in the fossil record. What they ended up finding, though, was quite spectacular and rocked the world of **paleoentomology**—the study of insects that focuses on fossil records.

When the scientists brought the rock sediment back to the lab, they dissolved it in special chemicals that eat away rock but leave behind organic material like pollen. The result is a black, goopy substance that they had

---

13. Fun fact: Cycads were around in the age of the dinosaurs and don't seem to have changed much.

to search through drop by drop. As they sifted through the gunk, they found something that knocked their socks off: insect wing scales. Remember that butterfly wings are covered in tiny scales that look like powder if they brush off onto your hand. The scientists realized that these scales belonged to ancient butterflies or moths that lived 200 million years ago, which predates the fossil evidence of kalligrammatids by about 35 million years. These scales are now the oldest evidence we have of **lepidoptera**—the order of insects that includes butterflies and moths.

Now, fishing out tiny scales from murky black goop is not an easy task. How in the world would you separate the scales from the gunk? Timo van Eldijk, one of the scientists who was tasked with this and who was a student at the time, was given a very curious tool: a dissection probe tipped with a single human nose hair. "The nose hair has just the right length and springiness for getting a pollen grain, or in this case a butterfly scale, to adhere to it," van Eldijk said. "I was just provided these by my professor, I don't know whose nose hair it was. It's probably best not to ask."

Thanks to that trusty nose hair, van Eldijk and his team fished out seventy scales or scale fragments.

Looking at them through an electron microscope, they discovered that about twenty were hollow. This provided another clue. Up until then, it was believed that ancient butterflies and moths had **mandibles**, which are pincerlike mouthparts that are used to chew. But today, just about every moth and butterfly with hollow scales has a long, straw-like proboscis that can slurp up liquid. This suggests that 200 million years ago, there were butterflies and moths fluttering around with proboscises, before there were any signs of flowering plants. It seems as though proboscises did not evolve alongside flowers, as scientists originally thought. Instead, ancient butterflies and moths that had a proboscis sucked up sugary droplets from nonflowering plants that made seeds.

It's so cool that a group of scientists who were originally digging deep into the ground for ancient pollen grains ended up finding prehistoric butterfly bits that provided a major breakthrough about how modern butterflies came to be. As a result, we had to rethink how butterflies and flowers evolved together. That's one of the great things about science: If we follow our curiosity, we never know what surprises are waiting around the corner.

## A MILLION-YEAR-OLD MIGRATION

We might not have any fossils of monarch butterflies, but that hasn't stopped scientists from figuring out how to trace their history. A few years ago, scientists realized they could use fancy new **genomic techniques** to unlock evolutionary clues that lie hidden within monarchs that exist today. **Genomics** is the study of all an animal's genes (the genome). In other words, it is the study of the complete set of an animal's DNA. Genomics looks at how the genes interact with one another and with the animal's environment. These techniques involve taking a bit of tissue from a butterfly's thorax (the middle part of the insect behind the head) and examining the DNA.

It turns out that monarch butterflies originally came from what is currently the southern United States and northern Mexico. They migrated each year like monarchs today, but their migration was a much shorter distance, maybe because milkweed wasn't spread out as far across the United States and Canada as it is now. Monarch butterflies have been migrating back and forth between what is now known as the United States and Mexico for at least *1 million years*. Our species, *Homo sapiens*, has been on the planet for only 300,000 years. So, the annual North American monarch migration is older than modern humans.

At some point in time, monarch butterflies spread out in three directions. Many stayed in the present-day United States and Mexico, but a number went south to Belize, Costa Rica, and into South America, as well as south Florida, Bermuda, and Puerto Rico. Other monarchs went west to Hawaii, Samoa, Fiji, New Caledonia, Australia, and New Zealand. Finally, a bunch of monarchs crossed the Atlantic Ocean, landing in Portugal, then Spain, and then Morocco. When did all this traveling happen? Some records show that European colonizers saw monarch butterflies in the Atlantic and Pacific areas in the mid-1800s. However, these were just sightings; the butterflies might have been there a long time before that. Sure enough, genomic testing suggests that monarchs spread out to the Atlantic and Pacific a lot earlier, as much as 2,000 to 3,000 years ago.

Scientists are still piecing together the full story of monarch butterflies. As genomic techniques and other technologies improve even further, their history will, hopefully, become even clearer. Wouldn't it be cool if someone reading this book (maybe even you!) one day makes a discovery about a monarch history-mystery?

Now let's turn from dinosaurs, nose hair probes, and the million-year-old migration to see where we can find monarchs around the world today.

## INTERNATIONAL SUPERSTARS

It is unfortunate that sometimes people become interested in a certain animal and start learning about them only when that animal is threatened with extinction. Scientists often have an easier time getting money from governments or other organizations for their research if the animal they want to study is in danger. This isn't always the case, but it happens often enough that it makes the system seem backward. Of course, it's good that animals in trouble can get the attention they need; it's just that it'd be better if we didn't have to "hurry up and study them" before they are gone.

All this is to say that we know more about where monarch butterflies exist in the world because they are in trouble. Specifically, the population of monarchs that overwinter in Mexico is becoming smaller and smaller, and the population of monarch butterflies in western North America has become catastrophically low. The situation has become so dire that Dr. Brower and other people petitioned the US Fish and

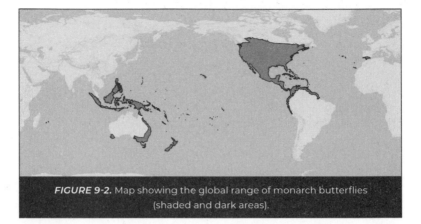

**FIGURE 9-2.** Map showing the global range of monarch butterflies (shaded and dark areas).

Wildlife Service to list monarch butterflies under the Endangered Species Act. This is a US federal law that protects all species threatened with extinction by making it illegal for people to harvest, keep, trade, or transport them. The law also requires that the species' habitat is protected. The US federal government provides money to states where species listed in the Endangered Species Act are found so they can enforce the law, conserve the habitat that the species needs, and generally make plans to save the species. So, listing monarch butterflies under the Endangered Species Act would be a big deal.

As part of the process, the US Fish and Wildlife Service had to do what is called a Species Status Assessment. This involves figuring out how the species as a whole is doing, including around the world and not just within the United States. So, three scientists at the US Fish and Wildlife Service—Dr. Kelly Nail, Dr. Kristen Voorhies, and Lara Drizd—looked for as many records of observations of monarch butterflies that they could find. They scoured scientific papers. They searched inaturalist.org, which is an online platform for scientists and citizens to post pictures and sightings of all kinds of plant and animal species. They also searched through flickr.com, a photo sharing site. In the end, the scientists identified seventy-four countries, islands, or island groups that had sightings of monarch butterflies since the year 2000 (see Figure 9-3). The team published a review of their findings in the scientific journal *Frontiers in Ecology and Evolution*.

One thing you'll notice if you look at the places in the table and on the map is that monarch butterflies have spread to much warmer places compared to where they originated in North America. Many of these places are tropical. In these new locations, there is no cold winter the monarchs need to escape from, so they can stay put all year and they don't need to migrate. Outside North America, many monarch butterflies breed year-round,

| Region | Country / Island / Island Group |
|---|---|
| Australia, New Zealand, and Indo-Pacific Islands | Australia, Commonwealth of the Northern Mariana Islands, Cook Islands, Federated States of Micronesia, Fiji, French Polynesia, Guam, Johnston Atoll, Kiribati, Marquesas Islands, Marshall Islands, Nauru, New Caledonia, New Zealand, Norfolk Island, Palau, Papua New Guinea, Réunion, Samoa, Society Islands, Solomon Islands, Tonga, Tuvalu, Vanuatu |
| Central America and Caribbean | Anguilla, Antigua and Barbuda, Bahamas, Barbados, Belize, Bermuda, Bonaire, Costa Rica, Cuba, Dominica, Dominican Republic, El Salvador, Grenada, Guadeloupe, Guatemala, Haiti, Honduras, Jamaica, Martinique, Nicaragua, Panama, Puerto Rico, Saba, Saint Kitts and Nevis, Saint Martin, Sint Eustatius, Sint Maarten, Turks and Caicos Islands, US Virgin Islands |
| Eastern North America | Canada (Eastern),* Mexico,* Saint Pierre and Miquelon, United States (Eastern)* |
| Hawaii | United States (Hawaii)* |
| Iberian Peninsula | Azores, Canary Islands, Gibraltar, Madeira, Morocco, Portugal, Spain |
| South America and Aruba | Aruba, Colombia, Curaçao, Ecuador, Guyana, Peru, Suriname, Trinidad and Tobago, Venezuela |
| Southern Florida | United States (Florida)* |
| Western North America | Canada (Western),* Mexico (Western),* United States (Western)* |

**FIGURE 9-3.** Countries where monarch butterflies have been sighted since the year 2000, grouped into eight worldwide regions. The asterisk (*) is placed beside countries that are listed in more than one.

including during that country's winter. This is very different from monarch butterflies in the eastern United States and Canada, where, as you'll remember from previous chapters, they breed in the spring, summer, and early fall.

Monarch butterflies that live in Australia and New Zealand are a little bit unique compared to monarchs in other parts of the world. In Australia, some monarch butterflies migrate, whereas some do not. In New South Wales, monarchs have been found to migrate up to 236 miles and roost for about two to four months in prickly-leaved paperbark trees and lantana shrubs. This migration is at a much smaller scale than that of North American monarchs. Remember that North American monarchs travel thousands of miles and overwinter for four to five months. In New Zealand, monarch butterflies don't migrate, but they form clusters in different types of trees. As we've learned, it makes sense that the butterflies would huddle together to keep warm when it gets a bit chilly.

An interesting difference between monarch butterflies around the world is that monarchs that migrate tend to have bigger wings than monarchs that don't migrate. Also, the farther the monarchs migrate, the redder their wing color tends to be. Scientists are really puzzled as to why migrating monarchs have redder wings. We can add this to the to-be-solved list of monarch mysteries.

One thing that monarch butterflies have in common, no matter where they live in the world, is that as caterpillars, they need milkweed. Milkweed is the only plant they will eat. So, it's no surprise that where there's milkweed in the world, there are also monarch butterflies. There are all different kinds of milkweed, and the type of milkweed found in one country might be quite different from the milkweed found in another. Also, some types of milkweed are not native to certain countries but instead were introduced. No matter what kind of milkweed a certain country or island might have, monarch butterflies seem to find it and the caterpillars eat it.

How did monarch butterflies end up scattered all over so many parts of the world? How did they cross the Atlantic and Pacific Oceans? That's a trip of 3,000 miles or more, with no land in between for pit stops. Scientists aren't entirely sure how monarchs did it, but they suspect that monarch butterflies *could* make pit stops in the middle of the ocean if they came across a ship. There are a number of reports from the 1800s of sailors seeing butterflies while out at sea. Monarch butterflies might have ridden on wind currents and hitchhiked on ships, and this combination of "wind-surfing" and hitchhiking might have eventually brought them to the other side of the ocean.[14]

These modes of travel might have helped monarch butterflies in the 1800s, but remember that genomic tests with monarch butterflies suggest that a number of monarchs left North America thousands of years before that. There were no big ships back then. It is possible that monarchs were carried solely by the wind or, as a few scientists suggest, by storms. Some monarch butterflies might have been swept up by hurricanes or cyclones and carried long distances—sort of like Dorothy and Toto being carried off in a tornado in *The Wonderful Wizard of Oz*.

As for the milkweed that the monarch butterflies would need in their new home, if the plants weren't intentionally planted there by people, then milkweed seeds probably traveled by wind, too. If you look at a milkweed seed, you'll see that it certainly seems built for wind

---

14. In the 1970 issue of their *Insect Migration Studies* newsletter, the Urquharts reported that a monarch tagged on September 25, 1968, by E. R. McDonald of Port Hope, Ontario, was recaptured forty-nine days later in Havana, Cuba. This butterfly would have flown about 2,000 miles, including 100 miles over water. The Urquharts questioned how the butterfly got there and suspected that it took advantage of the shipping between Florida and Cuba.

travel. The seed is attached to silky, parachute-shaped fluff, perfect for floating on the wind (see Figure 9-4).

So now that we have a better idea of where monarchs are found around the world, what happened with the US Fish and Wildlife Service's Species Status Assessment? Did monarch butterflies end up being listed under the Endangered Species Act? The answer is no, for now. The verdict, announced in December 2020, is that monarch butterflies qualify to be on the

**FIGURE 9-4.** A milkweed seed that I later planted in my garden.

endangered species list, but there are 161 other species that are in greater need of protection. Also, there are already a number of existing state and federal efforts that are trying to help monarch butterflies. Finally, Dr. Nail, Dr. Voorhies, and Drizd found that monarchs live in many other parts of the world. So, although the eastern and western North American populations of monarchs are in trouble (more on this in Chapter Ten), there are other populations around the globe to ensure the species doesn't go completely extinct. The US Fish and Wildlife Service decided that monarch butterflies will be put on a sort of "waiting list" to be classified as endangered. At least that's better than an outright no.

Hopefully, the people responsible for the endangered species list keep a few things in mind. First, we don't have a very good idea of how the monarchs are doing in the seventy-four different countries, islands, and island groups around the world. How big are their populations? Are the number of monarchs in each location decreasing over time, increasing, or staying the same? We simply don't know. It is quite a gamble to rely on populations of monarch butterflies whose statuses are unknown.

For example, Dr. Nail, Dr. Voorhies, and Drizd identified sixteen locations where monarchs had been seen in the past, but they had *not* been seen since 2000 (see Figure 9-5).

Why have there been no sightings of monarchs in these places for over twenty years? Why did the monarchs seemingly disappear? Did they not establish a firm population in these areas to begin with? Maybe they were just "passing by" and people happened to see them. Or maybe they did live in those places for a while and then something wiped them out. If this is the case, should we be concerned? Unfortunately, we may never know.

Another thing to keep in mind is that even though there might still be monarchs in other parts of the world, do we really want to allow the North American monarchs to become extinct? The annual migration to

| Region | Country / Island / Island Group |
|---|---|
| Australia, New Zealand, and Indo-Pacific Islands | American Samoa, Brunei, Indonesia, Malaysia, Mauritius, Philippines, Timor-Leste, Tokelau, Wallis and Futuna |
| Central America and Caribbean | British Virgin Islands, Cayman Islands, Montserrat, Saint Barthélemy, Saint Lucia, Saint Vincent and the Grenadines |
| South America and Aruba | French Guiana |

FIGURE 9-5. Countries where there is evidence of historical occupation of monarch butterflies, but no evidence has been found since the year 2000.

Mexico is one of the greatest migrations of any species on Earth. North American monarch butterflies outnumber monarchs elsewhere on the globe. Losing them would be a devastating hit to the species' population as a whole.

In October 2023, the International Union for Conservation of Nature (IUCN) downgraded the classification of the migratory monarch butterfly from endangered to vulnerable to extinction on its Red List of Threatened Species. This listing is separate from the Endangered Species Act in the United States, and it does not change any protections, rules, or laws concerning monarch butterflies. But it is still a call to action around the world that we need more funding for research projects and conservation efforts to continue to fuel the momentum of all the important work being done to help the species.

In the meantime, we shouldn't wait to help North American monarch butterflies. Scientists began ringing the alarm bells for them a long time ago. Let's take a closer look at how North American monarch butterflies are doing so that we have a clearer picture of the challenge that lies ahead of us and what we can do to help.

# CHAPTER TEN

# MONARCH EMERGENCIES

So far in this book, the spotlight has been on the eastern monarch butterfly population—the population of monarch butterflies that live east of the Rocky Mountains and that migrate over 2,000 miles to Mexico each fall. But if we look on the other side of the Rocky Mountains, along the western side of the United States, there's some monarch magic going on there as well. There are monarch butterflies that spend their spring and summer in states such as Nevada, Idaho, and Oregon. When it gets chilly in the fall, these butterflies migrate to the coast of California for the winter. Just like eastern monarch butterflies that fly to Mexico, these western monarchs spend the winter months hanging out in clusters of trees.

They tend to choose eucalyptus, Monterey cypress, and Monterey pine.

Despite being separated by the Rocky Mountains, the western and eastern monarch butterfly populations appear to be genetically identical. They do have a slight physical difference, though. If you place an eastern monarch butterfly and a western monarch butterfly side by side, you'll see that the eastern monarch has bigger forewings. This is probably because eastern monarchs tend to migrate about six times farther than western monarchs. Whereas some eastern monarchs fly as far as 2,000 miles, western monarchs fly about 310 miles on average.[15] That's still quite a distance for such small, seemingly delicate insects. Like monarchs that migrate to Mexico, among all the possible places they could choose to stay for the winter, western monarchs choose particular places with certain features. And different generations of monarchs come to the same spots each year. How do they know where to go? How do

---

15. Some recovered tags in Mexico have come from butterflies west of the Rocky Mountains, which suggests that instead of going to the California coast for the winter, some western monarchs make the trek all the way to Mexico. Scientists aren't sure how many do that. Although there haven't been any documented cases of monarchs flying from Mexico to the western United States in the spring, scientists suspect that it happens.

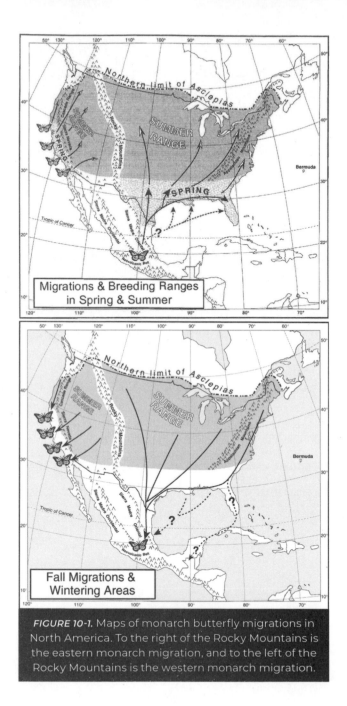

**FIGURE 10-1.** Maps of monarch butterfly migrations in North America. To the right of the Rocky Mountains is the eastern monarch migration, and to the left of the Rocky Mountains is the western monarch migration.

they know how to choose a safe overwintering site? It's incredible.

Compared to eastern monarch butterflies, western monarch butterflies have received less attention. However, Dr. Kingston Leong devoted his whole career to learning as much as he could about western monarchs. "Although their numbers at California winter sites is just a fraction of those of Mexican colonies," Dr. Leong said, "their clusters are still amazing to see and what a wonderment of nature that adults and children have treasured and appreciated." For over thirty years he has done field research on their winter gatherings to understand the "whys" of their overwintering behavior, and he has protected their winter survival through habitat management. Over time, he has learned some pretty cool things.

Like the eastern monarchs that migrate to Mexico, western monarch butterflies are quite picky about where they spend their winters. Before their population crashed in 2020–21, big clusters of overwintering western monarchs could be found along the California coastline from southern Mendocino County all the way south to Baja California, Mexico. The number of overwintering sites tended to vary from year to year, but generally ranged from 150 to over 250 sites. At each site, there could be anywhere from a few dozen butter-flies to several hundred thousand. Curiously, the sites with the most monarch butterflies tend to be on the central coast between Santa Cruz and Santa Barbara Counties (see Figure 10-2). Scientists weren't sure why monarch butterflies preferred the central coast, so Dr. Leong decided to find out.

Dr. Leong and his team looked at recordings of where monarch clusters were cited over a ten-year period, from 1990 to 2000. They also collected data from over 120 weather stations. They found that during winter, more northern parts of the California coastline tend to get more rain and have colder temperatures. The more southern parts of the coastline are too warm and don't get as much dew. The central California coastline seems to be the sweet spot. It has lots of morning dew and a high relative humidity, which stops the monarchs from drying out while they are roosting. The temperature is cold enough that monarchs can't fly, allowing them to conserve their energy, but it is warm enough that they don't freeze to death. There are even some warmer days when the monarchs can stretch their wings and fly a short distance to get a drink of water from a freshwater source. (They don't drink the salt water from the ocean—*blech!*)

Western monarch overwintering sites are found in **groves**: small groups of trees that don't have any under-brush. Monarchs tend to choose groves of eucalyptus

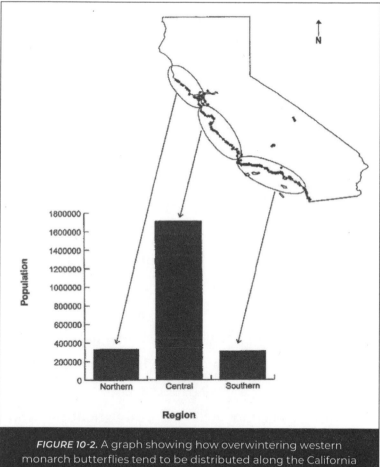

**FIGURE 10-2.** A graph showing how overwintering western monarch butterflies tend to be distributed along the California coastline from 1990 to 2000. The northern region is north of Santa Cruz County, the central region is from Santa Cruz County to Santa Barbara County, and the southern region is south of Santa Barbara County.

trees, Monterey cypress, or Monterey pine trees. These groves are on slopes that provide the best exposure to winter sunlight. Dr. Leong realized it's also important that these groves experience as little wind as possible. If the butterflies are blown off their perch throughout the winter by gusts of wind, they have to burn precious stored energy to fly back, or they have to look for a new place to stay. If the wind is colder than the air temperature, the monarchs will freeze to death. So, sunny, calm, cozy, cool groves are exactly what monarch butterflies need. They don't choose clustering sites randomly. Just like the oyamel fir trees in Mexico that we learned about in Chapter Five, groves near the central California coastline provide the ultimate microclimate for monarch butterflies to survive the winter.

However, western monarchs sometimes abandon their overwintering sites. Winds can be so strong that even the trees can't stop the monarchs from being disrupted. Dr. Leong called these abandoned sites **transitional sites**. Sites where monarchs stay throughout the whole winter and provide stable protection over a number of years are called **climax sites**. Bigger clusters of butterflies tend to be found at climax sites compared to transitional sites. Importantly, though, it is possible that climax sites can become transitional sites. Trees eventually become old and die, or they become diseased or infected with insects, or they are destroyed by natural disasters. They might be cut down or torn out by restorationists. Even if just a small number of trees disappear from a climax site, the monarch butterflies will lose protection. The empty space where the trees used to be will let in wind, rain, and colder temperatures. The site will become drafty. The climax site will then become a transitional site, or the butterflies will stop overwintering there completely.

On the other hand, transitional sites can become climax sites. Young trees that naturally start to grow in a grove or that are planted can grow into strong, wind-blocking protection for monarch butterflies. Strategic tree trimming can let in more sunlight. However, too much tree trimming, or tree trimming in the wrong spots, can compromise the microclimate for overwintering monarch butterflies.

Thanks to his many years studying overwintering sites along the California coastline, Dr. Leong is an expert on western monarch butterfly habitat management. He has helped maintain and create a number of crucial overwintering areas so that monarch butterflies can thrive. However, despite his hard work and expertise, and despite the fact that monarch butterflies are important for California's tourism economy (many people come to visit the monarchs each year), very few overwintering sites are protected. Many sites have been destroyed. From 2017 to around 2021, over a dozen sites were damaged with inappropriate tree trimming or removed to make way for houses, buildings, and other urban development. During that time, the western monarch population suffered a terrifying drop. The Morro Bay Golf Course, which hosted as many as 90,000 butterflies, had none during the winter of 2020–21. Volunteers reported that the only monarch butterflies they could find anywhere along the California coastline that winter were at Pismo Beach. There were only about 2,000 butterflies. In the 1980s, there were 4.5 million butterflies along the coast. Although the size of the western monarch population can fluctuate from year to year, such a significant drop is extremely alarming. Something is drastically wrong.

Western monarch overwintering sites could receive more protection if monarch butterflies become listed under the federal Endangered Species Act, or if they are listed as endangered under the California Endangered Species Act. A new law could also be created by the California state legislature to protect overwintering sites. As we saw in Chapter Nine, monarch butterflies have not yet been formally recognized as endangered species in the United States. Instead, they have been put on a waiting list. Let's hope the western monarchs don't disappear before the waiting is over. Or, better yet, let's hope that their dwindling population can bounce back.

## THE WESTERN MONARCH COUNT

The Western Monarch Count is a yearly effort to estimate the size of the western monarch population and keep track of how the butterflies are doing. It was originally called the Western Monarch Thanksgiving Count because volunteers would go out during the three weeks surrounding the Thanksgiving holiday. Then, a second count was added—the New Year's Count—which happens during three weeks around New Year's Day. Now both of these efforts are simply called the Western Monarch Count. The Western Monarch Count is organized by staff at the Xerces Society for Invertebrate Conservation (or the Xerces Society for short—pronounced *Zer-sees*) and longtime volunteer Mía Monroe.

How does the Western Monarch Count work? Counting monarch butterflies roosting way up in a tree is quite tricky, especially since the underside of their wings can be mistaken for dead leaves. "First, a volunteer goes to where clusters of monarchs have been seen in the past," Monroe explained. "We suggest that they do a 'scouting trip' during a sunny day midmorning, since the monarchs will be warming up and taking short flights from their clusters to find nectar and water. This helps give away where the roosting site is." Later in the day, the volunteer can return when the monarchs are roosting. Using binoculars, the volunteers take their time counting the butterflies in the cluster. Volunteers work in pairs so that they can compare their numbers. "It takes time," said Monroe. If there are similar clusters, the volunteers can multiply the total they counted from the one cluster by the number of similar clusters. Sometimes taking photos of the clusters helps, because volunteers can confirm their count at home when looking at the photo on their computer screen. "Volunteers go through training before they begin counting monarchs," said Monroe. "And in the end, we don't have an exact count of the butterflies, but we have a really good estimate."

"From my earliest years I have been a nature nut," Monroe remembered. "I have always loved butterflies, ferns, redwoods, tide pools, and hummingbirds. My parents encouraged me through a beautiful garden, camping that highlighted years with lots of wildflowers and meteor showers, and getting up early to see tortoises in the desert.

"My grandmother would come down on the train from San Francisco," Monroe continued, "and as a very small child, I'd gather milkweed along the tracks that had eggs on them to bring home to rear into butterflies. My grandmother took our family every year to Pacific Grove to see the overwintering butterflies. So, early on, I connected the seasonal arrival with the start of school, and the winter break with the butterflies here as a refuge."

Monroe became a national park ranger, and she played a major part in establishing the Western Monarch Count. Years ago, before the count was formally established, she heard that World Wildlife Fund donated money to the Xerces Society so they could do an "inventory" of all the places along the coast of California where monarchs had been known to spend the winter. She offered to help. "I was honored and thrilled to have my offer accepted," said Monroe. "Not only did I get to see the monarchs and help with the research, but I also had 'field time' with scientists who taught me how to find the monarchs, count the clusters, and understand the conditions they need.

"I learned that these scientists often went out in November each year to see the monarchs, and to conduct their own studies about monarch movement and health. I started to go out every year, too," said Monroe. "Soon, I became aware that what they were saying was true: The monarch population seemed to be declining and some sites were cut down to improve views, reduce hazard trees, or build new homes." There were big campaigns to help save the monarchs, such as Welcome Back Monarch Day and the Butterfly Parade at Pacific Grove, complete with butterfly cookies and orange pumpkin ice cream. "I was hooked," said Monroe.

People felt they should formalize what Monroe and the scientists were doing each year, along with the fun events. "It was time for a statewide count, with guidelines," recalled Monroe. "While organized and overseen by scientists, it would be a volunteer event. Plus, local people who knew the area could advocate for protection and share their knowledge with the public and schoolchildren. In 1997, the Western Monarch Thanksgiving Count was born."

The Western Monarch Count has grown in both the number of sites visited and the number of volunteers who participate. Monroe continues to be the regional coordinator, helping to organize the annual counts and train volunteers. She participates in the counts, too. "Although I got into this through my job as a park ranger," said Monroe, "most of my monitoring is as a proud Xerces Society volunteer."

Monroe and other volunteers with the Western Monarch Count have seen the tragic decline of the monarch population firsthand. "Yes, I have seen fewer and fewer monarchs," she said, "and it is shocking and depressing. There's a sense of urgency and concern about how overwhelming these changes are." What could be behind these changes?

## WHAT IS CAUSING THE CRISIS?

What is causing the tragic disappearance of western monarch butterflies? Scientists like Dr. Leong suspect that monarchs have been dealing with a number of problems for a while now and they are losing the battle. As we've seen, there are pesticides and herbicides, and milkweed has been eliminated in many areas. Then there's climate change, which is creating all kinds of problems, such as droughts. Lack of rain and hotter-than-usual temperatures cause nectar flowers, including milkweed, to dry up and die.

Wildfires might also play a part in the western monarch decline. Although wildfires have always been a part of the ecosystem of the western United States, in recent years they have been burning bigger and hotter than usual. Referring to the large wildfires that occurred in California in 2019 and 2020, Dr. Leong said, "The forest fires produced a smoke blanket that covered much of California for several weeks. Smoke from these forest fires may have stopped them from reaching the winter grounds." This idea stems from a small study that Dr. Leong did in the early 1990s, where he exposed overwintering monarch butterflies to smoke. "When exposed to smoke, the butterflies immediately drop to the ground," said Dr. Leong.[16] "I saw that the recovered butterflies clustered on other leaves within the grove but never on the leaves that had been exposed to smoke. This suggests that monarch butterflies are sensitive to smoke and will avoid it."

There is still much to learn about how wildfires affect monarch butterflies and other insect populations. If smoke from wildfires somehow contaminate

---

16. We saw this in Chapter Four, when one of Dr. Lincoln Brower's Mexican guides lit a bonfire to warm up, causing millions of monarch butterflies perched in the oyamel fir trees to drop to the ground.

the monarch butterflies' usual overwintering sites, perhaps they find other places to spend the winter. If they do, we can certainly hope that they manage to survive the cold winter months and that we will see them again soon. However, there have been no reports of monarch butterflies clustering in other places. This suggests that the state of the western monarch population is indeed incredibly grim.

In positive efforts, the Xerces Society has begun what they call a Western Monarch Call to Action. On their website (xerces.org/western-monarch-call-to-action), they describe the five top actions we can take right now to help the western monarch population bounce back. The Xerces Society recognizes that long-term efforts are needed to help the monarch population recover; but for now, their five steps can set the stage for long-term recovery efforts and help stop the butterflies from totally disappearing. Also, even though we still have a lot to learn about western monarch butterflies, the five steps are based on the available evidence and our current understanding of what stressors affect monarchs, and butterflies more generally. As the Xerces Society website states, if we wait until research gives us all the answers, the western monarchs might be gone. Here are the five steps that the Xerces Society recommends we take to help save western monarch butterflies:

1. Protect and manage California overwintering sites.
2. Restore breeding and migratory habitat in California. This includes planting native nectar flowers and milkweed. Flowers that bloom in the early spring, between February and April, are particularly important because adult monarchs will be very hungry after months of roosting in the overwintering sites.
3. Protect monarchs and their habitat from pesticides.
4. Protect, manage, and restore summer breeding and fall migration monarch habitat outside California.
5. Answer key research questions about how to best aid western monarch recovery.

The Xerces Society website gives details for each of these five steps so that people like you and me can pitch in and help, especially if you happen to live in California or in one of the surrounding states where the western monarchs spend their spring and summer.

As important as it is for us to take action, it is also important to remain hopeful. Monroe suggested a really good example: "There have been times after storms when I've been out with families looking for monarch butterflies. We gently pick up each drenched monarch, breathe our warm, human breath to dry them, and soon see them flutter away. What a sign of hope that we can each make a difference!"

Monroe also pointed out that monarchs, and other insects, are amazingly resilient. They evolved to migrate in order to adapt to change. For example, in California, they roost in eucalyptus trees, which are not actually native to the state but were introduced. She sees a glimmer of hope in the fact that monarch butterflies have not been listed under the Endangered Species Act. "The first thing they said in an announcement was the unprecedented groundswell of support and varied actions across the continent to help monarchs. People didn't wait for a decision or legal direction. Time was of the essence, and everyone was finding something they could do. I found this very inspiring and uplifting as I was sharing yet more difficult news about further steep, precipitous declines."

**FIGURE 10-3.** Monarch butterflies roosting on a eucalyptus tree.

Let's hope that the western monarch call to action gains more and more momentum. Perhaps if we all help, the western monarch butterfly can make an amazing comeback.

## EASTERN MONARCHS IN CRISIS, TOO

In 1980, the Mexican federal government declared that monarch butterflies would be protected in the country during the months when they were overwintering. Dr. Brower and others were concerned that this decree was too vague, because it left open the possibility that trees could be logged when the butterflies were not there. In addition, the decree ignored the fact that Indigenous and ejido communities had retained rights to that land since the 1930s. Dr. Brower and scientist Dr. Leonila Vázquez García came up with a plan that was nicknamed the "string of pearls." In this plan, the monarch butterfly roosting areas were the pearls, or "core zones," where logging and other extractive activities would be strictly forbidden. These core zones would be strung together by "buffer zones," where people could use natural resources within government rules. Dr. Brower and Dr. García thought that their string of pearls design would strike a balance between forest conservation and preexisting rights of Indigenous and ejido communities.

In the year 2000, the string of pearls areas were officially named the Monarch Butterfly Biosphere Reserve (we'll call it the Monarch Biosphere for short). The Monarch Biosphere is the size of almost 139,000 football fields, straddling the State of Michoacán and the State of México, about sixty-two miles northwest of Mexico City. The aim was, and still is, to protect the oyamel forests. As we saw in Chapter Five, the trees provide a special microclimate that allow monarch butterflies to survive the winter. The Monarch Biosphere is also a refuge for many species of birds, mammals, plants, and fungi. The region's basins also filter water for over 4.1 million people, and the forests generate oxygen. At the time the Monarch Biosphere was established, one of the biggest threats to the oyamel forests—and therefore to the monarch butterflies—was believed to be illegal logging. Pro Monarca thought that unchecked tourism also posed a threat. As a result, Pro Monarca did much work to oversee tourism at the overwintering sites, providing tourism-based jobs to ejido communities and establishing an ecotourism industry run by locals.

World Wildlife Fund also became highly involved

with the Monarch Biosphere. Each year, staff from World Wildlife Fund Mexico (WWF Mexico for short) work with local communities and partners to measure the size of the migratory eastern monarch butterfly population. How do they do it? A team goes out into the forests on foot, every two weeks, to find the outermost trees that the monarchs roost in. They record these locations and then "connect the dots" on a map to make a polygon. Then they measure the size of the polygon. The size of the polygon provides a measure of the area the monarchs are occupying in the forest, which is an estimate of the health of the eastern monarch migration. Bigger polygons mean a healthier monarch migration.

Studying the data collected from 1993–2021 shows that the estimated size of the eastern monarch butterfly migration has gone up and down from year to year, but overall, there has been a decline. Scientists estimate that about fifteen acres are necessary for the migration to be sustained over time. If the area dips below that number, the monarch migration might not be able to survive.

As alarming as these numbers are, it does not mean that monarch butterflies will become extinct. As we saw in Chapter Nine, monarch butterflies exist in other parts of the world. The declines displayed in the graph reflect the declining health of the monarch migration. As Dr. Lincoln Brower stated decades ago, the annual eastern monarch migration is "an endangered biological phenomenon."

Do we know why the eastern monarch butterfly migration is in danger? And if we do, what can we do to help?

## WHAT IS CAUSING THE CRISIS?

Removing trees from the overwintering sites disrupts the crucial microclimate the monarchs need to survive the winter, as we saw in Chapter Five. The forests become draftier and the butterflies are less sheltered from snow, rain, and wind. If the butterflies stay, they could freeze. If the butterflies choose to leave, where would they go? There might not be anywhere else on the continent that could protect the monarchs during winter. It is therefore crucial that the oyamel fir trees in the Monarch Biosphere are preserved and protected.

Figure 10-4 shows that between the years 2001 and 2007 there was a steady increase in illegal logging, followed by a steep decline in 2007–09. The total area of forest cover loss was about 3,665 football fields! The Mexican federal government cracked down on this logging. After that, the main cause of forest cover loss was climate-related factors like rain and wind (except a blip in 2013–15).

Despite the decline in illegal logging in the Monarch Biosphere, it still happens. In their 2021 press release, WWF Mexico stated that "clandestine logging" is still a serious threat to the forests. (*Clandestine* describes something done in secret.) Remember that the Monarch Biosphere includes land that has been owned collectively by ejidos and Indigenous communities since the 1930s. What has been called clandestine logging includes

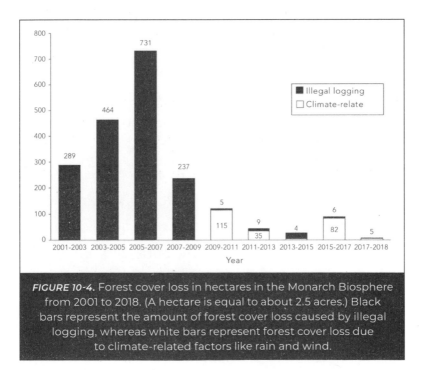

**FIGURE 10-4.** Forest cover loss in hectares in the Monarch Biosphere from 2001 to 2018. (A hectare is equal to about 2.5 acres.) Black bars represent the amount of forest cover loss caused by illegal logging, whereas white bars represent forest cover loss due to climate-related factors like rain and wind.

logging done by people who have a right to use natural resources in that area. However, the area occupied by monarch butterflies in the Monarch Biosphere has continued to shrink despite the steep decline in illegal logging. There must be more to the story of why the eastern monarch migration is in trouble.

Forests can be **degraded** due to a number of reasons. **Forest degradation** means that a forest still exists, but it is a shell of what it once was. It is caused when a forest is ravaged by unsustainable or illegal logging, storms, fires, pests, or disease. A degraded forest can no longer support wildlife as it once did. **Deforestation** is a different concept, one that refers to clearing a forest to put something else in its place, such as fields of food crops. Trees continue to be lost in the Monarch Biosphere due to wind, drought, and legal logging that is done to control pest insects that can damage and kill trees. Some scientists are urging that to get a full picture of the eastern monarch butterfly decline, however, we need to look outside Mexico. We need to consider the butterfly's entire habitat, which includes their breeding grounds. And where are their breeding grounds? Mostly in the vast amount of land in the United States that has been converted to monocultures to feed millions of people.

As we saw in Chapter Six, milkweed has been practically wiped out from corn and soybean fields. We can plant milkweed to replace what has been lost to cropland, but things might not be so simple. Dr. Carl Stenoien and his team discovered that when milkweed grows naturally, the plants are usually spaced apart, creating a low-density habitat for monarchs. When people plant milkweed intentionally in nature strips, gardens, or elsewhere, the plants end up being clumped and close together in patches, creating a high-density habitat.[17] Monarch butterflies tend to lay more eggs per milkweed plant in these high-density habitats, and there is *less* chance that the caterpillars will survive. Survival rates for monarch caterpillars are much better when milkweed plants are spaced out and fewer eggs are laid per plant. Remember Dr. Kelsey Fisher's research in Chapter Seven where she attached radio transmitters to individual butterflies to track their movements? I bet in the future, her research or similar research by others will provide insights into where and how we can best plant milkweed.

---

17. When planting milkweed, it is important to plant species of milkweed that are native (that is, grow naturally) in your area. Otherwise, there is the possibility of spreading parasites or interfering with the monarchs' migratory behavior. The Xerces Society has some great resources about native milkweed found across North America.

It is easy to target and blame illegal loggers, and even to blame another country. It is a lot harder and more uncomfortable to look at our own agricultural practices and the policies that support them, realize the harm we may be doing, and try to change the way we do things. Especially when billion-dollar pest control companies are involved. It's certainly not impossible to make changes for the better, but it likely won't be easy. One thing history has shown us is that sometimes the very best things in life come with a struggle (sometimes a very hard struggle). In the end, however, the struggle ends up being 100 percent worth it. The monarch butterflies, and all the other insects and animals that can benefit from more sustainable agricultural practices, are worth it. Don't you agree?

Great things can happen when creativity is applied to problems, especially when the creativity of different people is allowed to mingle. We can apply our creativity to the plight of monarch butterflies, to learn more about them and to help them, whether we are scientists or volunteers.

## CHAPTER ELEVEN

# LIVING NEAR THE MONARCHY

Homero Aridjis, the boy who years ago watched with wonder as rivers of monarch butterflies streamed through the streets of his village, grew up to be a famous writer and poet. He has written about monarch butterflies and the overwintering grounds he visited as a child. His descriptions paint a vivid picture of what it must be like to experience the monarch-filled forests:

> Atop Altamirano, the butterflies were there, a million-strong colony in the sun-swept patches of the ancient crater. Making waves in the air, they gave the dark green grove an undulating rhythm of its own. They also came

in bursts of living fire, vibrating in sheaves of orangey-black beams.

Each tree was a splendor in itself, an animated world, a rain of winged tigers: rooted in time, it seemed suspended, at once distant and near.

Myriad butterflies piled up, shifted, opening and closing above the trees, or hung in live clusters from the branches that bent under their weight. From fir to fir, from plant to plant, their numbers grew; flittering nervously, they alighted on sunlit paths of the forest floor.

Spellbound, I didn't know where to look first, at the clusters hanging from the branches or the butterflies like flying leaves against the light. The monarchs were a sonata and with my eyes I listened to their music.

Aridjis remembered that millions of monarch butterflies would arrive at his village of Contepec and the nearby forests each year on November 1 and 2, like clockwork. As he pointed out, the annual arrival of the monarch butterflies has great cultural significance for the people of Mexico, because it coincides with their celebration of **Día de los Muertos**, the Day of the Dead.

"Local people thought that the butterflies were the souls of dead people or their own families who were returning to the earth in the shape of the butterflies."

## MORE THAN A MIGRATORY INSECT

Día de los Muertos is celebrated each year in Mexico on November 1 and 2. On these days, it is believed that the souls of deceased loved ones are carried by monarch butterflies to visit the living for one night.[18] November 1 is usually reserved for remembering children who have died, whereas November 2 is for remembering adults. Día de los Muertos is often confused with Halloween, which is celebrated on October 31, but the two events are very different. Halloween is considered a dark night associated with fright, terror, mischief-making, and trick-or-treating. Día de los Muertos, on the other hand, is a day filled with color, joy, and love and respect for the dead. It is a celebration of life. Indigenous people in Mexico believe that death does not end life, but rather new life comes from death. An example of this is the life cycle of food crops: A new crop grows each year from

---

18. Some scholars believe this isn't quite true, and that it was likely invented in the 1980s to promote butterfly tourism. See pbs.org/wgbh/nova/video/misinformation-monarch-butterflies.

*FIGURE 11-1.* People dressed as monarch butterflies during a parade in Mexico City to celebrate the Day of the Dead.

the previous year's crop that lies buried in the ground. In this way, Día de los Muertos is also associated with the harvest. Some large cities in Mexico hold parades as part of the celebration of life and death.

The most central symbol of Día de los Muertos is the **ofrenda**: an altar that families construct to honor their deceased loved ones. They decorate the ofrenda with photos of the departed and some of their personal belongings as reminders of their life. Ofrendas can also be decorated with sugar skulls, or **calaveras de azúcar**. Rather than being morbid or scary, these skulls are bright and colorful and are meant to represent the cycle of life.

Besides being a tribute to the departed, another purpose of the ofrenda is to provide what the dead need in order to complete their journey to visit the living. This is represented by the four elements: water, wind, earth, and fire. Water is placed in a pitcher on or near the ofrenda so that the returning spirit can quench its thirst. Traditional paper banners, called **papel picado**, represents wind.[19] Food, often in the form of bread, represents earth. Finally, candles represent fire. They are often placed in the form of a cross to represent the four compass directions so the returning spirits can find their way.

Ofrendas are very colorful, vibrant, and quite beautiful. Much of their color comes from the **cempasúchil**, a type of marigold flower found in Mexico that is used to decorate ofrendas, as well as the graves of those who have died. *Cempasúchil* comes from the Nahuatl word *cempohualxochitl* ("twenty-flower"). By placing cempasúchil on an ofrenda, both the vibrant color and the strong scent are meant to help create a path for spirits to lead them to their family's home. The orange of the

---

19. Mexicas (people we now call Aztecs) and other Indigenous people in Mexico invented the practice of making papel picado by creating ceremonial carvings with bark paper, which the Nahuatl called amatl (Mexican Spanish: amate).

**FIGURE 11-2.** An ofrenda decorated with calaveras de azúcar, papel picado, and cempasúchil.

flower is thought to match the orange of the monarch butterfly. Even today, when asked whether they believe monarch butterflies carry the souls of their departed loved ones, some Mexican people have answered, "Well, it makes sense because butterflies are orange, just as the same flowers that we use in Mexico."

Besides being a powerful symbol for Día de los Muertos, monarch butterflies have been represented by some Mexican people as harvesters. For example, before Spain colonized Mexico, the Mazahua and Otomí peoples recognized that the arrival of the monarchs each winter coincided with the end of the harvest, and so they incorporated monarch butterflies into their rituals of gratitude and requests for a good agricultural cycle. For the Mazahua, the monarch butterfly was entwined with the Sun God, who is the creator and giver of life. It was said that during the winter season, the sun's rays were transformed into butterflies, which were seeds of the sun. They covered the earth and people, fertilized the soil, pollinated the flowers, and "adorned life and air." When the monarchs departed at the beginning of spring, the Mazahua people saw this as a sign to prepare the soil and begin sowing for the next cycle of crops.

## SAVING THE MONARCHS

As Homero Aridjis grew older, he worried that the beautiful orange-and-black flying insects he saw as a child, which are so closely entwined with Mexican culture and history, were in danger. So in 1985, he founded the Grupo de los Cien (Group of 100), a group of artists and intellectuals who gathered to raise awareness of environmental problems in Mexico. "One of my worries, always," remembered Aridjis, "was that I saw the deforestation. We had politicians, loggers destroying the forest and I didn't want the hill of my village to have the same fate." Aridjis said he became a committed environmentalist. "I wanted to save the hill of my village. And because it was the symbol of the monarch butterflies, I wanted to protect also the monarch butterflies."

In 1986, the Grupo de los Cien asked the president of Mexico to declare the habitat of the overwintering butterflies as protected sanctuaries. The president agreed, and that October, five areas were declared protected sites. However, illegal logging continued and local people kept cutting down trees. "I wrote many, many articles in the newspapers and I made many calls to stop the logging," said Aridjis.

He didn't give up. Aridjis became the Mexican ambassador to the Netherlands, Switzerland, and then to UNESCO (the United Nations Educational, Scientific and Cultural Organization). As a result of his determination and hard work, the Monarch Biosphere became a UNESCO World Heritage Site in 2008. "When I was an ambassador to UNESCO," recalled Aridjis, "one of my ambitions—private ambition—was to get UNESCO to declare the sanctuaries in Mexico a Natural Heritage of Humanity. And before I was leaving UNESCO, the committee approved the monarch butterfly sanctuaries as protected Natural Heritage of Humanity."

Throughout his crusade to save the monarch butterfly and the land where he grew up, Aridjis didn't dwell on the fact that he was "just a poet." "Because I am a poet," said Aridjis, "sometimes the people in Mexico didn't pay much attention to me. They thought I was a little crazy. They said, 'Oh, he is a poet. He is irresponsible.' And I was happy that they considered me irresponsible and a little crazy because I was very direct in my fight."

Aridjis pointed out that in addition to environmental activism, the butterflies were a continual inspiration for his writing. "I know that poetry is not very popular in the way that you can't make money," said Aridjis, "but I love poetry, and the environment, for me, is the poetry of life."

Tragically, for years now, the monarch butterflies have stopped arriving in Aridjis's childhood village of Contepec. He described the overwintering colonies at remaining sites as "pitiful remnants of their former splendor." As we've seen, despite over thirty years of conservation efforts, monarchs are still in trouble. Maybe we need to take a hard look at the conservation efforts themselves? This is a question that researchers like Dr. Columba González-Duarte are asking.

## WHAT ABOUT THE PEOPLE?

Dr. Columba González-Duarte is a professor at Mount Saint Vincent University in Halifax, Canada. She has studied the knowledge of Indigenous Mexican communities who share a habitat with overwintering monarch butterflies. She learned that monarchs are more than a migratory insect; they are an integral part of powerful human traditions. Monarchs have profound meaning beyond their biology and behavior. As we will see later in this chapter, Dr. González-Duarte's work, along with Indigenous ecological knowledge, is important for monarch butterfly conservation efforts.

Dr. González-Duarte is an anthropologist, which means she studies human beings, their societies, and their culture. To do her research, she uses a method called **ethnography**. This is a type of fieldwork where she completely immerses herself in the everyday life of the people she is studying. At the same time, she tries to remain an observer so she can later describe what she learned. What's really cool about Dr. González-Duarte is that she studies **interspecies ethnography**: how humans relate to other animals, and how other animals relate to humans.

How did Dr. González-Duarte end up studying monarch butterflies and monarch butterfly conservation? After graduating from Universidad de las Américas, Puebla, Mexico, Dr. González-Duarte went to the University of Toronto, in Canada, to earn her PhD. She was interested in how species move, and she wanted to incorporate Canada somehow in her fieldwork. Monarch butterflies seemed to be the perfect fit, as they encompass the three countries that Dr. González-Duarte was familiar with: Mexico, the United States, and Canada. She realized she would have to include the Monarch Biosphere in her research, considering that is where the eastern monarchs overwinter each year.

Dr. González-Duarte conducted many interviews with government and nongovernment workers and community members. She spent many days observing four communities who had restricted access to the forest where they live. What follows is what she uncovered about monarch butterfly conservation through the establishment of the Monarch Biosphere, using the lens of ethnography.

When the Monarch Biosphere was first established, logging and all human trespassing was banned in the core zones. Although this law was well intentioned, people were living on that land. These people, as a community, had been using the upper mountain ranges sustainably, such as harvesting mushrooms and cutting down a tree now and then for heat and cooking. The lower hills were divided into family plots where traditional food gardens called **milpas** were grown.[20] Milpas have been used in Mexican and Central American culture since ancient times. The creation of the Monarch Biosphere changed all this. For six months of the year, these communities could no longer access the forests. They could use only a few of their milpas. However, they needed both the forests

---

20. *Milpa* comes from *milpan*, a Nahuatl term meaning "fields."

and milpas for survival. A number of the communities protested by burning and logging their own plots, and some even sabotaged their neighbors' land. In this way, the conservation laws backfired. The oyamel trees, the monarch butterflies, and the people were less protected.

Declaring the core zones of the Monarch Biosphere "human-free" led to another big problem: increased organized crime. Organized criminal groups have used the nature reserve as a route through which they can smuggle humans, drugs, weapons, plants, and animals. In response, both government and nongovernment organizations (NGOs for short) have provided money to pay for armed people to patrol and secure the Monarch Biosphere. Some of these people are local residents from the communities who live on the reserve. Dr. González-Duarte found that these local residents are sometimes mistakenly identified as "narco-trespassers," people involved with illegal drug activity who trespass through the reserve. In reality, people being paid to patrol the area are only trying to make a living. Being in an area with very few jobs, they might have been forced into their "security guard" role. These patrollers end up being both the cause and the victims of violence when they encounter criminal activity in the forest. Another way that some people on the reserve have tried to avoid poverty is to participate in the organized crime taking place on their land. Often, there are few alternatives.

Depending on who you talk to, the idea of organized crime in the Monarch Biosphere is controversial. For example, Dr. Sharp lived at the entry of the Cerro Pelón Monarch Butterfly Sanctuary for eight years, where she ran a butterfly ecotourism business and a nonprofit forest conservation effort, Butterflies & Their People. She argues that administrators of the Monarch Biosphere use "organized crime" as an excuse not to intervene in the logging. However, CEPANAF forest rangers in Cerro Pelón know that loggers "are not dangerous, just desperate—and young." Dr. Sharp interviewed Patricio "Pato" Moreno Rojas, a CEPANAF ranger who started working in Cerro Pelón in 2014. He said most loggers they encounter are unemployed twelve- or fourteen-year-old kids who are no longer in school. "They are not [dangerous] . . . they are simply scared," Pato said. "We're wearing our uniform, but it is not a police uniform—it's a uniform of park guards—but people are scared. We know that they are unarmed. There is no organized crime in this place."

Pato views clandestine logging as a result of desperation, since "timber provides cash."

Avocado plantations are another problem that has emerged over time in the Monarch Biosphere. Over the past few years, avocados have surged in popularity across North America. According to the US Department of Agriculture, since 2001 avocado consumption has tripled, and by 2018 it was up to eight pounds per person. That is the weight of an average housecat. Although the United States produces its own avocados (mainly in California), to meet year-round demand, the US imports avocados from other countries. Mexico has become the dominant supplier, providing 89 percent of avocado imports in 2018.

With the increase in demand for avocados, avocado plantations began popping up in the Monarch Biosphere. Avocados themselves aren't illegal, but the clearing of protected oyamel trees to plant them is. Even more complicated is that some members of local communities have been extorted by members of organized crime: They have been pressured by criminals to develop and run avocado plantations, and in exchange the criminals will provide them with protection from rival criminal organizations. The degree to which communities are involved with this "avocado crime" varies. However, as Dr. González-Duarte pointed out, the problem underlines the fact that communities can no longer manage their land themselves because of the restrictions imposed on them through the establishment of the Monarch Biosphere.

In the year 2000, some of the restrictions in the Monarch Biosphere were loosened, but communities were still forbidden to use and manage the forest. Tourism was allowed, which helped to provide a bit of income for some community members. However, it does not occur at every overwintering site, resulting in an uneven opportunity for residents. Also, it can greatly affect the forest. Local people have tried very hard to operate tourism in environmentally friendly ways, but with massive numbers of visitors each year to their impoverished region, it's impossible *not* to leave an ecological footprint. For example, together Homero Aridjis and Dr. Lincoln Brower visited the Piedra Herrada overwintering site in the State of México one February. They saw a welcoming sign that read *No more than twenty people in the sanctuary*. However, they counted twenty-four tourist *buses* in the parking lot. If you are struggling to make enough money to feed your family, and throngs of people are willing to pay you to see the butterflies, wouldn't it be tempting to bend the rules?

The Mexican government made an attempt to assist the Indigenous and local people who live in the Monarch Biosphere, since they are now forbidden from using the forest to make a living and support themselves like they once did. In partnership with NGOs, they offer something called **payments for ecosystem services**, or PES for short. Basically, local residents are paid to conserve the land. This allows the government and NGOs to replace income they had taken away from residents, and it lessens the frustration and anger residents feel about losing their right to manage their land and log the forest sustainably. At the same time, the forest would be protected. Surely, it's a win–win situation for everyone, including the butterflies?

Unfortunately, no. The PES system has, in many respects, backfired. Residents receive PES only if there has been no or very little change to their land. At one point, the cutoff to receive PES was a 3 percent change to the forest: If more than 3 percent of the trees on their land had been cut down, the people living there received no money. In theory, fewer trees being cut down means monarch butterflies are being protected.

However, it was mostly members of organized crime who were cutting down the trees, not the residents. Dr. González-Duarte found that PES was denied even when a community cited that they were dealing with illegal logging. So, if residents wanted to receive their PES, which was usually the only money they could get to support themselves, they had to stop the illegal loggers. Local residents began organizing community forest patrolling practices. If illegal loggers were armed, the community patrollers were putting their lives at risk.[21] Dr. González-Duarte pointed out that the organizations who fund the PES system are aware that this is happening. However, they are still holding the residents accountable for any loss of trees on their land. In this way, through the PES program, the government and NGOs are indirectly paying the local residents to patrol the forest and take life-threatening risks.

Another way that the PES system has backfired is that the money goes directly to **ejidatarios**. These are people who have inherited an ejido—usually men, and usually inherited from father to youngest son. They hold the title to that land and they act as a leader for

---

21. As we saw earlier, CEPANAF rangers at Cerro Pelón would disagree: In their experience, illegal loggers are never armed.

that ejido. Dr. Sharp and Dr. Wright pointed out that ejidatarios make up only about 10 to 15 percent of the population who live on the land. Ejidatarios decide how to use the PES, whether that involves distributing it to the community or keeping the money for themselves. In this way, PES are undemocratic and patriarchal.

Taking all of this together, what started out as a strategy to protect the monarch butterfly has unraveled into human poverty and, arguably, crime and violence. On top of that, the size of the monarch butterfly migration continues to decline. On the surface, it might make sense for international conservation programs to forbid human presence during the monarch butterfly's overwintering period. It might also make sense to pay the residents to compensate for the restrictions being imposed on them. Even better, these payments can be based on how well the people protect the forest. However, research by Dr. González-Duarte, Dr. Sharp, and Dr. Wright shows that such a strategy denies the fact that people live in that forest, have lived there for generations, and depend on that forest to survive. According to Dr. González-Duarte, an unfortunate outcome of introducing "human-free zones" for the butterflies is that organized crime saw this as an opportunity. If there are no humans around, then illegal activities go undetected. Criminals have basically taken over the land. When these illegal activities include logging, residents have to put their lives in danger to stop the logging so they can be paid and put food on the table. It is a serious dilemma.

In the previous chapter, we saw the decline in illegal logging in the Monarch Biosphere over the years. However, it's more complicated than that, because it depends on who you talk to. For instance, in their 2013 *New York Times* article, Dr. Lincoln Brower and Homero Aridjis claimed that reports showing that illegal logging in the reserve has been reduced to almost zero are "incomplete and misleading." They argued that these reports consider only certain parts of the reserve and do not capture "selective" logging, where only a few individual trees have been removed. Even removing just a few trees in an area can alter the forest microclimate, increasing the chance that the monarchs will starve or freeze to death.

In 2020, the COVID-19 pandemic hit, and people around the world were told to stay home to stop the spread of the virus. Businesses closed. Many workers in Mexican cities were laid off and went home to the countryside, where there were no jobs. Because of the pandemic, the monarch sanctuaries were closed to tourists, which put even more residents out of work.

While living near the Cerro Pelón Monarch Butterfly Sanctuary, Dr. Sharp noticed an increase in logging during COVID-19. Recently, she said, "When people get desperate, there's always a buyer for black market wood poached from the protected area. It got so bad that I couldn't go hiking without running into one of my neighbors dragging down a tree." She heard one community member say that it's hard to care about butterflies when you're hungry. Clearly, the complexity of the situation goes well beyond the monarchs.

At the time this book was published, we didn't know the full extent of the impact of the COVID-19 pandemic and its economic slowdown on illegal logging and the forests where the monarch butterflies overwinter. From Dr. Sharp's eyewitness accounts, the pandemic only worsened the situation. It is very important to stress, however, that the local residents of the Monarch Biosphere are not simply trying to make a fast buck. Like the people who established the Monarch Biosphere in the first place, they want to protect the forests. After all, their people have been a part of the forests for generations. They have been put in a complicated situation with little help and few answers.

## "SAD TREES"

After listening to the people who live on the land now known as the Monarch Biosphere, Dr. González-Duarte realized that their concept of a healthy forest is very different from what some conservation programs consider to be "healthy." Instead of a forest without humans, Indigenous and local people have always seen themselves as *part* of the forest. When Dr. Brower and Dr. García designed their string of pearls plan for the Monarch Biosphere with core and buffer zones, they recognized that the Indigenous and local people are an important part of the forest ecology. As previously discussed, these people had rights to that land since the 1930s. However, the establishment of the Monarch Biosphere stripped the people of those rights. Local ejidos and Indigenous communities no longer had power to make management decisions. The issue, Dr. Wright pointed out, is that "there is unequal power between conservationists and campesinos."[22]

Also, conservation programs have considered the forest

---

22. Campesinos is a name given to peasant farmers in Spanish-speaking regions.

in the mountains to be separate from the land below; after all, monarch butterflies roost for the winter up in the forest and not in the valleys. However, people who have lived there since ancient times view the forests and the valleys as intricately connected. For generations, Indigenous and local people have dedicated the lower land to their milpas, or family corn gardens. The upper forests are seen as the providers of water, wood, edible plants and mushrooms, and animals to hunt. Together, the milpas and the forests form an ecosystem that supports humans, and humans in turn support the ecosystem through caring for the land, trees, and other life that lives there. Trees *can* be cut down sustainably, to make way for new trees and to provide humans with heat and fuel. Plants and mushrooms can be sustainably harvested. Animals can be hunted sustainably, too. The communities take only what they need. In this way, humans help keep the populations of other species at healthy numbers. Like the rest of nature, humans are a vital component that support the cycle of life.

Another insight from the people who have lived on the land now known as the Monarch Biosphere is that we don't need to compartmentalize our interactions with the natural environment. Using the land does not need to be thought of as separate from our knowledge, worldviews, and appreciation of the land. Everything we do, think, and feel about the land can occur at the same time and blend together. This is what Dr. González-Duarte refers to as a "ritualized view of the two ecological niches": the lower land and the upper forests. The Indigenous and local people's rituals and ceremonies recognize the sacred energy that flows between their milpas and the upper forests. They also recognize the interconnectedness of nature and other aspects of life. They connect the lower and upper lands and recognize the role of the land as provider. Historical documents from many of the communities show that misfortune has come to those who neglect their obligation to give recognition and thanks to the land through ritual and ceremony.

Dr. González-Duarte emphasized that the Indigenous and local people's activities in the forest are rooted in an appreciation for the sacred value of the forest and a sense of reciprocity with other living creatures. Their traditional activities support a healthy forest. She stated that the Monarch Biosphere conservation model misses this entirely. Separating land into "human" and "human-free" zones has created a rift between humans and nature, and has provided an opportunity for organized crime to sneak in.

One of the ancient rituals that has been seriously affected by the explosion of organized crime in the Monarch Biosphere is what is called community **rondas**, or walks. It is a community service known as **rondas del buen orden**, which is unpaid community work that is meant to "give back" to the forest. Dr. González-Duarte discovered that this practice was very successful in conserving the forest long before the Monarch Biosphere conservation program began. Unfortunately, these rondas are now often done to combat organized crime, and they can be extremely risky for community members. In some cases, people have stopped performing rondas or even visiting the upper forest to perform their ritual practices because it is now simply too dangerous. "I've been there with these people," recalled Dr. González-Duarte, "and it's scary to find loggers who are armed."

Finally, Dr. González-Duarte has observed that the Monarch Biosphere conservation program has focused only on land where monarch butterflies over-winter. It has ignored other land, and has even created a "forced disregard" for places where there are no monarch butterflies. This has become more of a problem over time because as the size of the monarch migration declines, fewer trees host the butterflies. Indigenous and local people who live on the land now called the Monarch Biosphere told her that where there are no monarch butterflies, the forest is filled with "trees, yet *sad trees*." They explained that trees need humans to look after them. With no human intervention, the trees become unhealthy, such as suffering from plagues or disease, and therefore are sad. It is ironic that in this way, the Monarch Biosphere conservation program is having quite the opposite effect of what it is meant to do: It is creating "sad" trees instead of nurturing and conserving healthy, "happy" trees.

The situation at the monarch overwintering grounds is very grave indeed. Decades ago, Aridjis and his Grupo de los Cien wanted to save the monarch butterfly out of love for the environment and the land where he grew up. They certainly did not intend to spread violence and crime, and they certainly did not intend to throw the Indigenous and local people into poverty and desperation. What lessons, if any, can we take from what has happened? Is there any way to turn things around?

## WHAT CAN WE DO?

After witnessing the terrifying conditions in the Mexican forests and the hardships that Indigenous and local people are enduring, Dr. González-Duarte realized that protecting monarch butterflies means taking care of people, too. We need healthy habitats for the butterflies and for their human neighbors. The idea of conservation has always implied that nature needs to be protected from humans and that nature is isolated and different from us. "What my research tells me," said Dr. González-Duarte, "is that actually humans need to be part of that nature. They need to be in that nature to be able to actually protect it in a meaningful way." Humans, after all, are animals, too. We live on the earth just like all other species.

Despite all our advances in technology, and despite how different humans might seem from other animals, humans are part of nature. Indigenous peoples have always known this. "It's important to recognize Indigenous knowledge," Dr. González-Duarte explained. "That is something that has not happened from any authority: international, national, or local. We have Indigenous knowledge that will be meaningful knowledge to protect this reserve." A very important aspect of this knowledge is that it does not focus on one species or one phenomenon. Learning about monarch butterflies from an Indigenous point of view also means learning about the forest, the mushrooms, the water, and everything else. There is no knowledge that is just about butterflies, or just about humans. "One thing we see often across Indigenous groups," said Dr. González-Duarte, "is that they don't see a single species as their species. My research suggests that protecting this butterfly means protecting a whole complex, healthy environment for many other species that could be less charismatic." These other species could include insects or predators that are not usually considered "cute" or "beautiful" like monarch butterflies. Conservation organizations often focus on protecting one species. "They don't find the same sort of language from Indigenous groups who are not interested in protecting one butterfly; they want to protect their forest and their habitat and their home."

Dr. González-Duarte believes that the dangerous and complex situation in Mexico is a cue for us to start opening up to the idea of Indigenous knowledge as a different way to conserve the environment. "This doesn't mean that we don't need other forms of knowledge, like

Western science," Dr. González-Duarte emphasized. "But we have other alternative ways of thinking. Our highly focused form of conserving is not working. It has been in place for over twenty-five years, and we don't have better numbers."

Dr. Wright added that Indigenous knowledge matters only when ejidos and Indigenous communities have the power to make decisions. "It's one thing to integrate knowledge. It's another thing to share authority." Are outsiders making decisions about the Monarch Biosphere on their behalf? If so, policies should be changed to reflect what we learn.

People have been resistant to consider Indigenous knowledge because they don't see it as a science, or they see it as something to incorporate *into* Western science. Dr. González-Duarte believes we have to break away from this way of thinking. Western science is not more valid than Indigenous knowledge, and vice versa. "We need to understand that Indigenous knowledge is scientific as well," she said. "It may follow other methods, but it has the history of knowing and trying through centuries of living in that land." The Indigenous scholar Dr. Gregory Cajete refers to Indigenous knowledge as "native science." This, Dr. González-Duarte believes, is a step in the right direction. "We have to see Indigenous knowledge as another form of science, and that it complements the Western science we are familiar with. They do not oppose each other."

Another reason why Indigenous knowledge has been disregarded or ignored boils down to deeply rooted bias and prejudices against certain people. This can be traced back to when European colonizers first came to North America and their narrow-minded beliefs that they were "superior" to the people who were already living on the land. This applies not only to the Spanish who colonized present-day Mexico but also to the Europeans who colonized present-day Canada and the United States. We saw this prejudice back in Chapter Three, when Catalina Trail, who discovered the monarch overwintering grounds, was dismissed as the "bright and delightful Mexican, Cathy." Dr. González-Duarte explained that when developing conservation programs, scientists often feel they can tell Indigenous people to behave in certain ways. "It's a clearly disrespectful way of seeing their form of life." It also assumes that Indigenous people are harming the environment. Dr. González-Duarte said that she has been in meetings where monarch butterflies were considered more important than people. Hierarchies have been placed between different kinds of humans, and between humans and the environment. "I think that's the main narrative that we need to contest when we are rethinking what conservation is going to look like in the future," she said.

And it's not just conservation scientists who need to examine their own bias and prejudices about conserving the monarch butterfly. People in general have been quick to blame or label those who appear to have no environmental ethics or who appear to be causing the extinction of the monarch butterfly migration. "We definitely have to stop criminalizing peasants in Mexico, assuming that, 'Oh, they cut the trees, they are bad people,'" said Dr. González-Duarte. "I hear this all the time. We need to understand that if they cut a tree, there's many, multiple different reasons why they find themselves in need of doing that." She acknowledged that we can be a part of those reasons, too. "We have the avocado here, we have our genetically modified corn, we have our activities that are forcing them to sometimes cut down the trees that the butterfly needs." Many people have pointed their fingers at the people of Mexico when they see the decline in the monarch butterfly population. And even within Mexico, fingers have been pointed to particular groups of people. But how might those of us who live outside Mexico be contributing to the problem?

Dr. González-Duarte said that the theme of "heroes versus villains" popped up quite a bit while she was examining her data. Conservationists, amateurs, or citizen scientists in Canada and the United States who raise monarch butterflies and campaign to save them are often seen as the "heroes." On the other hand, tree loggers in Mexico are viewed as the "villains." In fact, she often found that the amateurs refer to themselves as "crusaders," which further underlines their hero status. In her interviews, these heroes and villains expressed disgust for each other: The amateurs are disgusted by the tree loggers when they cut down trees in the Monarch Biosphere, and the tree loggers are disgusted by the amateurs' excessive care and investment in the monarch butterfly's survival. Amateurs also tend to see tree loggers as ignorant of the magnificence of the butterfly, whereas the tree loggers view monarchs as a part of the forest. Western science, too, is often seen as the hero in the story. Who exactly is the hero and who is the villain can shift depending on your point of view—and depending on who gets to tell the story. For instance, are amateurs the heroes, or are they in some ways the villains? At times, Dr. González-Duarte herself felt that she couldn't escape the theme of heroes and villains. "If I criticize conservation efforts and draw attention to people on the reserve, I'm seen as a villain who does not care about the protection of monarch butterflies. But if I focus on monarch butterflies, I'm seen as a villain who does not care about or account for the people."

These heroes and villains in the story of the monarch butterfly have certainly been at odds with each other. The people in the north and south have very different ideas about how the butterfly should live. Fundamentally, however, they want the same thing: They want the monarch butterfly to survive. Perhaps, as Dr. González-Duarte described, "The monarch can be seen as an actor who can bring together two worlds."

Blame has been launched across countries for a while. As we saw in Chapter Ten, at first illegal logging in Mexico was an explanation for the declining monarch butterfly population. Then people realized that milkweed has been wiped out from cornfields across the United States and Canada. "We have shifts in blame," Dr. González-Duarte said. "The blame is not on one side, yet we have been doing that. 'Oh, for ten years, the problem was in Mexico, the next ten years, the problem is in the United States.' It's shifting our eyes to others, instead of seeing our own actions and the ways we can intervene in our local communities and state." Blaming countries also distracts us from examining the specific policies, companies, people, and powers that are contributing to the problem, regardless of which country they come from.

In the end, as Dr. González-Duarte pointed out, the monarch butterfly needs a healthy habitat across its breeding grounds and along its migratory route. It needs milkweed, but it also needs nectar, water, and a forest. "It's not just about planting milkweed any longer," she said. "That's not going to do it. The sad part is, it's not going to do it." The three countries—Canada, the United States, and Mexico—together need to shift to a conservation model that doesn't focus just on how to conserve locally but on how to protect habitats and corridors across countries and across distant geographies. Protection must also extend beyond monarch butterflies to people and all other species as a whole. "That's the next challenge, I think," said Dr. González-Duarte "for conservationists and especially for this butterfly."

Dr. González-Duarte's research suggests that to help monarch butterflies, we need to be open to new ways of thinking. We need to revise conservation plans, enact policy change, and examine and address our biases and prejudices. This requires the cooperation of Canadian, American, and Mexican governments. This is a very complex challenge and there's lots of work involved.

As we tackle the tough challenges, there are small things we can do at the same time to help. One of these things is to act locally. Although we need to consider the planet as a whole with all its inhabitants when we are devising conservation strategies, doing things locally can add up over time to create broad changes. "I think it's important to call attention to protect your butterfly, your milkweed, your nectar, your water, the pesticides and herbicides being used where you live," Dr. González-Duarte said. "If you have a healthy population in Canada and the US, then there will be a healthy population in Mexico." This applies to people, monarchs, and populations of other species, too.

Dr. González-Duarte noted that the monarch butterfly is very resilient. It has rebounded and survived in situations where people thought it was doomed. "When we had a big storm in Mexico that killed many of them, people were thinking, 'Oh, they're not going to rebound. There's so few numbers now.' But they did. So there's a resiliency in this insect, which I don't think is unique of the monarch, but millions of other species, too, and that gives me hope." She also realizes that so many humans care about monarch butterflies, care *for* them, and love them. "So many people are heavily involved in wanting this species to survive so that gives me hope."

However, one thing that is worrying to Dr. González-Duarte is that we don't have a model to protect the butterflies or their migration. "If we want them to survive, we have to transition to a radically different model and that takes time." She knows that climate change has become much more of an issue over the last decade or so. "I think we're all doing our best," she said. "Scientists, social scientists, communities—we're all trying, and that's good. And sometimes the unexpected happens, so I am hopeful."

It is hopeful knowing that there are scientists like Dr. González-Duarte who are devoting their careers to understanding the world and making it a better place. Take all the scientists who are featured in this book: They care deeply about the survival of the monarch butterfly. In addition, research teams in Canada are starting to bridge Indigenous knowledge and Western science to gain insights about how to sustainably manage fisheries and how to keep healthy populations of caribou and musk ox in the Arctic. They have been using a framework called Etuaptmumk, which is Mi'kmaw for **Two-Eyed Seeing**. Mi'kmaw Elder Dr. Albert Marshall described it as "learning to see from one eye with the strengths of Indigenous knowledges and ways of knowing, and from the other eye with the strengths of mainstream knowledges and ways of knowing, and to use both these eyes together, for the benefit of all." So far, with the fisheries and Arctic species, the Two-Eyed Seeing framework is showing much potential.

Will Two-Eyed Seeing provide us with the fresh perspective on conservation that is desperately needed? Only time will tell. In the meantime, let's all hope, more than ever, that the "winged tigers" that Homero Aridjis described in his writings can hang on, be patient, and be strong.

# MORE THAN A BUTTERFLY

It is late June in southern Ontario. On the underside of a park bench hangs a tiny jade chrysalis with a thin strip of gold across the top. It looks like a piece of jewelry someone tucked under the bench for safekeeping. Indeed, it is about the size of an earring or a pendant that can hang from a necklace.

For about a week the chrysalis hangs there. People come and go, sitting on the bench to rest, reflect, or chat with the person sitting beside them. A small, scruffy dog on a leash gently sniffs the chrysalis. Otherwise, it hangs unnoticed.

Gradually, the jade color of the chrysalis fades. It becomes a transparent skin, revealing the black-and-orange pattern of the monarch butterfly wings that are folded up inside. Early one morning, the clear skin splits and crumpled wings burst out. The butterfly hangs upside down, its thin black legs clinging to the torn, empty shell that once held it safely inside. After a few minutes the butterfly's wings have stiffened and flattened, and the butterfly opens and closes them. A man sitting on the bench, sipping from his coffee cup, is oblivious to the orange-and-black display occurring underneath him. The butterfly opens and closes its wings some more. Open, close, open, close.

In a blink, the monarch butterfly lifts off. It flaps and floats out from under the bench and up into the air. The man startles. A small boy walking with his mother sees the butterfly and squeals with delight, pointing at it. The butterfly flies up, up, and lands in a tree, partially hidden by the green leaves.

This monarch butterfly—a female—will eventually mate and lay eggs. In the early fall, long after she has passed away, her descendants will make the long trek down through the United States and into Mexico. Those that survive will tuck themselves close between thousands of other monarch butterflies, wings folded like pages in a book, clinging to stately oyamel fir trees in the Mexican mountains. There, they will wait out the winter. At the same time, some monarch butterflies will cluster in trees along the western coastline of the United States. Others won't wait out winter at all, but rather, will enjoy warm, tropical weather year-round. Monarch butterflies found in pockets of Australia and New Zealand will wait out their winter in trees, too, but they will not migrate nearly as far as the monarch butterflies found in eastern North America.

The female monarch butterfly who is sitting up in the tree is more than a butterfly. She is the embodiment of the wonder and resiliency of nature. She is part of an annual migration older than the existence of modern humans. She began as an egg the size of a pinhead, and grew from a chubby caterpillar into an orange-and-black beauty. She can make blue jays barf if they try to eat her. She can navigate in this complex world that humans keep modifying more and more, for better or worse, and she can still find food and shelter. She is the descendant of millions of monarch butterflies that lived before her, and she is the ancestor of (hopefully) millions of monarchs that will live after her.

She is an essential part of the ecosystem. She pollinates plants and she is food for certain birds and mice.

Her presence alone shows the beauty of biodiversity and she is a sign of a healthy ecosystem.

She is also the embodiment of a rich and complex story. Her kind has captivated the human imagination, sparked wonder, and fueled passion in those who wish to understand her. People have spent countless hours watching, recording, experimenting, and even devoting their entire career to knowing the monarch butterfly inside and out. Does she know that her kind has been the focus of international scientific study? Does she know that monarch butterflies like her have inspired artists and scientists for generations? That thousands of citizens around the world have been recruited for decades to help understand the monarch butterfly's epic migration? That teams of scientists spent months camping in the Mexican forests to uncover why the forests are so special? From MRI machines used to peek inside the chrysalis, to high-powered slingshots, to radio transmitters, and to mini flight simulators, humans have funneled creativity and innovation to uncover the secrets of monarch butterflies.

The story she embodies also includes tension and conflict. She serves as a memory of squabbling scientists who were eager to discover the secret location of the monarch overwintering grounds. She represents the blame that has been passed between conservationists and Mexican tree loggers, and the discrimination faced by Catalina Trail and other people. Does the butterfly have any idea that her mesmerizing black-and-orange wing pattern is so deeply entwined in human history, in nature conservation, and in human culture? That since ancient times, she has been revered by many Mexican people as the embodiment of those who have died and who are honored each year? Through the lens of human experience, the monarch butterfly is a complex creature on many levels.

More than just a butterfly, the monarch inspires reflection and hope. If so much biological and evolutionary detail can be found in a monarch butterfly, what about all the other insects, animals, and plants that share this planet? Many are not as showy and beautiful as these "winged tigers," but they have incredible lives and secrets of their own. The intricate relationship that monarch butterflies have with milkweed, nectar flowers, and trees also reminds us that the ecosystem is a detailed, flourishing web of which so many creatures play a part. Human actions are upsetting this flourishing, as evidenced by the steep decline in the western and eastern monarch butterfly populations, as well as declines in many other species.

Yet there is opportunity and hope to guide the future of monarch butterflies, as seen through initiatives like Monarch Watch, Journey North, the Monarch Larva Monitoring Project, incorporating Indigenous knowledge, and the framework of Two-Eyed Seeing. If we listen, open our minds, and work hard, there is hope that more chapters about the monarch butterfly will be written. Maybe it's possible that rivers of monarch butterflies will flow down through Altamirano Hill once again.

# AUTHOR'S NOTE

I am writing this note in March 2023, and I am thrilled to report that the population of eastern monarch butterflies went up—at least a bit. In 2022, World Wildlife Fund and the other organizations it works with reported that ten overwintering colonies were found, which covered a total area of seven acres. This is a 35 percent increase from the year before. This uptick in the eastern monarch population happened despite a drought in the Upper Midwest of the United States in 2021 and extremely high temperatures in July and August in that region. The resiliency of monarch butterflies is incredible. However, we need to be cautiously optimistic, since this does not guarantee that the population is recovering. I encourage you to follow the Monarch Watch blog (monarchwatch.org/subscribe) or Monarch Joint Venture (monarchjointventure.org /blog) to keep up to date with the status of eastern monarch butterflies.

In more good news, the 2022 Western Monarch Thanksgiving Count had a final tally of 335,479 butterflies. This is up from a record low of less than 2,000 butterflies in 2020 and almost 250,000 butterflies in 2021. Amazing! Scientists were amazed, too. This increase shows the importance of ongoing efforts to help recover the western monarch butterfly population. But again, we must be cautiously optimistic. The population of western monarch butterflies is still far below what it was back in the 1980s, and the monarchs are vulnerable to extreme weather events. Heavy rains in 2022 caused flooding, downed tree limbs, and uprooted trees in overwintering grounds along the California coast. We need to continue our efforts and keep learning. You can stay updated on the status of the western monarch butterfly population at westernmonarchcount.org.

If you would like to be a part of the monarch butterfly recovery efforts, consider sending your sightings to Journey North (journeynorth.org). You can volunteer with the Monarch Larva Monitoring Project (monarch jointventure.org/our-work/monarch-larva-monitoring -project-online-training), and/or help Monarch Watch by tagging monarch butterflies in the late summer and early fall (monarchwatch.org). While helping scientists track, monitor, and learn more about monarch butterflies, you'll find out what it's like to do science and fieldwork if you're interested in becoming a scientist. Plus, you'll be making a difference. If you live on the West Coast, you might consider volunteering with the Western Monarch Count. There are other organizations you can discover, too. Volunteering to maintain community gardens in your neighborhood is another great way to help monarch butterflies and other insects. If the gardens don't have milkweed, perhaps you can talk to the community group about planting some that are native to where you live?

I am fortunate to live in an area where monarch butterflies live for part of the year. Last spring my daughter and I found a monarch egg underneath a milkweed leaf and we brought the leaf and egg home. We watched as the egg hatched into a tiny caterpillar, then grew, and finally transformed into a butterfly. I encourage you to do this if you can. It is one thing to read about metamorphosis, such as the description I provide in Chapter One, but it is quite another to watch its wonders unfold before your eyes. If you do find an egg and want to raise it, Carol Pasternak's book *How to Raise Monarch Butterflies: A Step-By-Step Guide for Kids* is an excellent resource. Perhaps you can incorporate raising monarch butterflies into a school science project? I must note, however, that experts do not recommend that people breed and raise monarch butterflies in large numbers, because this has the potential to spread disease to the butterflies and potentially to other insects.

Whether or not you live in an area with monarch butterflies, I highly recommend you visit a garden, meadow, or park, and take five or ten minutes to just watch and listen. Even if you live in a city, this can include spending some time observing the flowers in your backyard or a flower box on your apartment balcony. Many cities now have community gardens that anyone can visit. If you spend some time observing flower patches, you might be surprised by the diversity of life that you see. Maybe you can take a notebook with you and jot down descriptions of what you see, hear, and smell. The buzzes of bees and other flying insects (do they all sound the same?), the beetles and bugs, the colors, shapes, and sizes of their bodies, the different scents of the flowers, what the insects do on the flowers . . . You can also take time to notice the plants. Are there certain plants where insects gather the most? What variety of plants are there? Perhaps you can sketch what you see. Take a few moments to allow yourself to feel a connection to the land, the natural world around you, and the feeling that you are a part of that world, too. No matter how busy life gets, taking time out to be with nature now and then is totally worth it.

I also encourage you to be creative and think about other ways to help monarch butterflies. You can think big or small, and you can *do* big or *do* small. Here's a biggie that I hope you will consider: Is there a way to apply your passion, dreams, and future career path so that you can help the environment at the same time? Maybe you're passionate about monarch butterflies, or insects or animals in general, or maybe you're passionate about something completely different, like cars or computers or politics or fashion design. What can you do with it? Every bit you do counts. *You* count. I can't wait to see what you have in store for us!

# GLOSSARY

**abdomen:** the last body part of an insect that comes after the thorax; the abdomen of monarch butterflies is long and slender (plural: abdomens)

**agronomy:** a branch of agriculture that focuses on field-crop production and soil management

**angiosperms:** flowering plants

**animal cognition:** an area of science that explores how nonhuman animals think, learn, remember, make decisions, and solve problems

**automimicry:** when a member of a species imitates other members of the species, often for protection; for example, all monarch caterpillars have the same warning coloration, despite some caterpillars not being poisonous because of the type of milkweed they eat

**calaveras de azúcar:** sugar skulls that are bright, colorful, and meant as symbols to represent the cycle of life during Día de los Muertos

**cardenolides:** the poisons found in milkweed and other plants; at the right dose, they are used as a heart medication for humans

**carnivore:** an animal that eats meat (the flesh of animals)

**cempasúchil:** a bright orange, fragrant marigold flower found in Mexico that is used to decorate ofrendas, as well as the graves of those who have died, during Día de los Muertos; *cempasúchil* comes from the Nahuatl or Mexica (Aztec) word *cempohualxochitl* ("twenty-flower")

**central complex:** a cluster of cells in the monarch butterfly brain that is thought to be where the butterfly's internal compass is located

**chemical ecology:** the study of how organisms interact with their environment and other organisms through naturally occurring chemicals

**chemoreceptors:** sense organs of animals that allow them to detect certain chemicals; for example, our taste buds on our tongue are chemoreceptors

**chorion:** the outer shell of a butterfly egg; it protects the developing larva (caterpillar) inside

**chrysalis:** the outer protective covering that a caterpillar forms before transforming into a butterfly; the chrysalis of a monarch butterfly is bright green

**citizen science:** the public's contribution of observations and data to scientist-led projects and research; Monarch Watch and Journey North are examples of citizen science programs

**climax sites:** the name that Dr. Kingston Leong gave to overwintering locations along the coast of California where monarch butterflies remain throughout the winter; climax sites provide stable protection for the butterflies over a number of years

**cycads:** also called sago palms, these are a type of gymnosperm that look like squat palm trees

**deforestation:** clearing a forest to put something else in its place, such as fields of food crops

**degraded** or **forest degradation:** when a forest still exists but is in much worse shape than it used to be; a degraded forest can no longer support wildlife as it once did; degradation can be caused by unsustainable or illegal logging, storms, fires, pests, or disease

**Día de los Muertos:** the Day of the Dead, which is recognized each year in Mexico on November 1 and 2, to honor deceased loved ones and celebrate the cycle of life and death

**ejidatario:** a person who has inherited an ejido, holds the title to that land, and acts as a leader for that ejido

**ejido:** communal land in Mexico where people live and farm

**entomology:** the study of insects

**ethnography:** a type of fieldwork in which a scientist completely immerses themself in the everyday life of the people they are studying; they try to remain an observer so they can later describe what they learned

**exoskeleton:** the hard, shell-like outer surface of an insect

**flavonoids:** certain chemicals in plants that help create the bright colors of fruits and vegetables; milkweed contains flavonoids that glow purple under ultraviolet (UV) light

**frass:** caterpillar or insect poop

**genomics:** the study of all of an animal's genes (the genome), meaning the study of the complete set of an animal's DNA; genomics looks at how the genes interact with one another and with the animal's environment

**genomic techniques:** methods scientists use to study genomics; genomic techniques have been used to try to uncover the mystery of the evolution of monarch butterflies

**glyphosate:** a chemical that kills unwanted grasses and plants; its brand name is Roundup

**groves:** small groups of trees that don't have any underbrush

**guardabosques:** forest rangers

**gymnosperms:** plants that produce cones, such as pine trees and spruce trees

**herbicide:** a chemical that kills unwanted grasses and plants

**herbicide-resistant crops:** crops that have been genetically engineered to survive after chemicals called herbicides are applied to the crop to kill unwanted plants

**herbivores:** animals that eat plants

**instar:** the space of time between two molts of a caterpillar; monarch caterpillars experience five instars before becoming an adult butterfly

**interspecies ethnography:** the study of how humans relate to other animals, and how other animals relate to humans

**invertebrate:** animals without a spine or backbone, such as insects and spiders

**kalligrammatid lacewings:** a type of prehistoric insect found in fossils that is thought to be the ancestor of modern butterflies

**larva:** the wormlike, wingless creature that hatches from an egg laid by a monarch butterfly; also called a caterpillar (plural: larvae)

**latex:** a thick, sticky, white liquid that oozes from milkweed leaves if the leaves are punctured or otherwise injured; depending on the type of milkweed, latex contains poisonous chemicals called cardenolides

**lepidoptera:** the order of insects that includes butterflies and moths; taxonomy classifies living things according to domain, kingdom, phylum, class, order, family, genus, and species

**magnetic resonance imaging (MRI):** technology that uses a magnetic field and computer-generated radio waves to create pictures of the bones, internal organs, and other tissues inside our bodies

**magnetite:** a magnetic mineral that naturally occurs in some animals, such as monarch butterflies, homing pigeons, and dolphins

**mandibles:** pincerlike mouthparts certain insects have that enable them to chew

**mechanoreceptors:** sense organs of animals that enable them to detect touch, pressure, and vibrations; for example, we have mechanoreceptors in our skin

**metamorphosis:** an abrupt change in the structure of an animal as it develops; monarch butterflies go through four stages of metamorphosis: egg, caterpillar (larva), pupa (chrysalis), and butterfly

**microclimate:** the temperature, wind, and precipitation of a small or restricted area that differs from that of the surrounding area

**migration mortality hypothesis:** the idea that the population of eastern monarch butterflies is declining because many butterflies die during their annual fall migration to Mexico

**milkweed limitation hypothesis:** the idea that the population of eastern monarch butterflies is declining because there is less milkweed available where the butterflies can lay their eggs and the larvae can eat the leaves

**milpas:** traditional food gardens used in Mexican and Central American culture since ancient times; the word *milpa* comes from *milpan*, a Nahuatl term meaning "fields"

**molting:** the process of a monarch caterpillar shedding its skin; it can also refer to other animals' occasional loss of their feathers, shell, or outer skin

**monoculture:** the growth of only one type of crop or plant, such as corn, in a large space of land; monocultures end up replacing wild plants that pollinators and other animals rely on for food and habitat

**nectar:** the sugary liquid in flowers that is food for insects and other animals

**ofrenda:** an altar that families construct and decorate to honor their deceased loved ones; a central symbol of Día de los Muertos

**ovipositor:** a special organ insects have that allows them to lay eggs

**oyamel fir tree:** a type of tree found in the mountains of Mexico, upon which monarch butterflies roost during the winter; the word *oyamel* comes from the Nahuatl word *oyametl*

**pace:** how long it takes to cover a specific distance; it is different from speed, which is the distance covered in a specific amount of time

**paleoentomology:** the study of fossil records of insects

**papel picado:** traditional paper banners that symbolize wind during Día de los Muertos; Mexica (Aztecs) and other

Indigenous people in Mexico invented the practice of making papel picado by creating ceremonial carvings with bark paper, which the Nahuatl called amatl (Mexican Spanish: amate)

**payments for ecosystem services (PES):** money that people who live in or near the Monarch Butterfly Biosphere Reserve in Mexico receive if they preserve the forest

**pheromones:** a chemical substance that an animal gives off to influence the behavior of other members of its species; for example, butterflies give off pheromones that tell other butterflies that they are ready to mate

**predation:** when one organism kills and eats another organism

**proboscis:** the long, tubelike tongue of some insects that enables them to suck up nectar from flowers

**pupa:** the stage between a caterpillar (larva) and a butterfly; the pupa is what is inside a chrysalis before it is a fully developed butterfly (plural: pupae)

**pupate:** the process of becoming a pupa; when a larva, or caterpillar, forms a protective outer covering before transforming into an adult insect; in monarch butterflies, this involves forming a chrysalis

**radio antenna:** a component of radio telemetry; it is a device that a researcher holds that detects signals from the radio transmitter worn by the animal being tracked

**radio receiver:** a component of radio telemetry; it is a device that a researcher holds that turns the signals from the radio transmitter and radio antenna into beeps, which enables the researcher to determine the location of the animal being tracked

**radio telemetry:** tracking animals' movements using a radio transmitter, a radio antenna, and a radio receiver

**radio transmitter:** a component of radio telemetry; it is a device that an animal wears that sends out an invisible radio signal

**range:** the area within which an animal lives

**release-recapture line (RRL):** the straight line on a map between the location where a monarch butterfly was tagged and set free and the location where the butterfly was later sighted

**resin:** the sticky, gooey substance secreted by many trees that hardens to become amber; sometimes insects become trapped in resin and are preserved in amber

**rondas:** traditional walks performed by the local residents in Mexico who live in or near the Monarch Butterfly Biosphere Reserve; they are meant as a practice to conserve the forest

**rondas del buen orden:** unpaid community work done by local residents in Mexico who live in or near the Monarch Butterfly Biosphere Reserve; it is meant as a way to "give back" to the forest

**roost** or **roosting site:** a group of monarch butterflies that cluster close together, often in tree branches; monarch butterflies often roost overnight

**scanning electron microscope:** a high-powered microscope that uses an electron beam to create extremely magnified, detailed images

**sequestration:** the ability of an animal to store a poison in its body and not become sick

**single sweep hypothesis:** the idea that each spring, monarch butterflies leave Mexico and repopulate the United States and Canada in one wave or "swoop"

**successive brood hypothesis:** the idea that it takes more than one generation of monarch butterflies to repopulate the United States and Canada each spring

**sun angle at solar noon (SASN):** the angle between the sun and the ground when the sun is at its highest point in the day; it is believed to be a cue that eastern monarch butterflies use when they migrate to Mexico

**tentacles:** in monarch butterflies, the two black, antennae-like structures on a monarch caterpillar's head

**theory:** a possible explanation for something that needs to be tested

**thermochrons:** small, button-shaped devices that can measure and record air temperature

**thorax:** the middle part of an insect's body, where its legs and wings are attached (plural: thoraxes)

**trachea:** breathing tubes in an animal

**transitional sites:** the name Dr. Kingston Leong gave to coastal California overwintering locations that monarch butterflies abandon at some point during the winter

**trichomes:** hairs that cover the surface of milkweed leaves; monarch caterpillars need to shave these off before biting the leaf

**Two-Eyed Seeing:** a framework that Elder Dr. Albert Marshall described as "learning to see from one eye with the strengths of Indigenous knowledges and ways of knowing, and from the other eye with the strengths of mainstream knowledges and ways of knowing, and to use both these eyes together, for the benefit of all"

**vertebrates:** animals with a backbone

**weed:** an unwanted grass or plant

# REFERENCES

## BOOKS

Agrawal, Anurag. *Monarchs and Milkweed: A Migrating Butterfly, a Poisonous Plant, and Their Remarkable Story of Coevolution*. Princeton: Princeton University Press, 2017.

Cajete, Gregory. *Native Science: Natural Laws of Interdependence*. Santa Fe, NM: Clear Light Publishers, 2000.

Oberhauser, Karen S., and Michelle J. Solensky, eds. *The Monarch Butterfly: Biology and Conservation*. Ithaca, NY: Cornell University Press, 2004.

Pasternak, Carol. *How to Raise Monarch Butterflies: A Step-by-Step Guide for Kids*. New York: Firefly Books, 2012.

Urquhart, Fred A. *The Monarch Butterfly: International Traveler*. Chicago: Nelson-Hall, 1987.

## BOOK CHAPTERS

Howard, Elizabeth, and Andrew K. Davis. "Documenting the Spring Movements of Monarch Butterflies with Journey North, a Citizen Science Program." (Oberhauser and Solensky, 105–14.)

Leong, Kingston L. H., Walter H. Sakai, Walter Bremer, Dan Feuerstein, and Gwen Yoshimura. "Analysis of the Pattern of Distribution and Abundance of Monarch Overwintering Sites along the California Coastline." (Oberhauser and Solensky, 177–85.)

Malcolm, Stephen B., Barbara J. Cockrell, and Lincoln P. Brower. "Spring Recolonization of Eastern North America by the Monarch Butterfly: Successive Brood or Single Sweep Migration?" In Stephen B. Malcolm and Myron P. Zalucki, eds. *Biology and Conservation of the Monarch Butterfly*, 253–67. Los Angeles: Natural History Museum of Los Angeles County, 1993.

Oberhauser, Karen S. "Overview of Monarch Breeding Biology." (Oberhauser and Solensky, 3–7.*)*

Pierce, Amanda A., Sonia Altizer, Nicola L. Chamberlain, Marcus R. Kronforst, and Jacobus C. de Roode. "Unraveling the Mysteries of Monarch Migration and Global Dispersal through Molecular Genetic Techniques." Oberhauser and Solensky, 257–67.)

Zalucki, Myron P., and Wayne A. Rochester. "Spatial and Temporal Population Dynamics of Monarchs Down-Under: Lessons for North America." (Oberhauser and Solensky, 219–28.)

## ENCYCLOPEDIA ARTICLES

*Encyclopedia Britannica Online*, s. v. "Anthropology," accessed June 29, 2021, https://www.britannica.com/science/anthropology.

*Encyclopedia Britannica Online*, s. v. "Day of the Dead," accessed January 26, 2020, https://www.britannica.com/topic/Day-of-the-Dead.

*Encyclopedia Britannica Online*, s. v. "Endangered Species Act," accessed April 8, 2021, https://www.britannica.com/topic/Endangered-Species-Act.

*Encyclopedia Britannica Online*, s. v. "Ethnography," accessed June 29, 2021, https://www.britannica.com/science/ethnography.

Wright, Will. "Monarch Butterfly Conservation (Mexico)." *Oxford Research Encyclopedias, Latin American History*, published online September 15, 2022. Accessed January 21, 2022, from https://doi.org/10.1093/acrefore/9780199366439.013.1084.

## MAGAZINE AND NEWSPAPER ARTICLES

Aridjis, Homero. "The Ascent of Butterfly Mountain." Translated by Betty Ferber. *Orion Magazine*, September/October 2009. Accessed June 22, 2021, from https://orionmagazine.org/article/the-ascent-of-butterfly-mountain/.

Aridjis, Homero. "Last Call for Monarchs." *Huffington Post*, December 6, 2017. Accessed June 17, 2021, from https://www.huffpost.com/entry/mexico-monarch-butterfly-migration-_b_4745915.

Brower, Lincoln P. "Ecological Chemistry." *Scientific American* 220, no. 2 (1969): 22–29.

Brower, Lincoln P. "Monarch Migration." *Natural History* 86 (1977): 40–53.

Brower, Lincoln P., and Homero Aridjis. "The Winter of the Monarch." *New York Times*, March 15, 2013. Accessed June 17, 2021, from https://www.nytimes.com/2013/03/16/opinion/the-dying-of-the-monarch-butterflies.html.

Dale, Daniel. "Couple's Home Was Butterfly Ground Zero." *Toronto Star*, April 18, 2009. Accessed February 19, 2020, from https://www.thestar.com/news/gta/2009/04/18/couples_home_was_butterfly_ground_zero.html.

Machemer, Theresa. "Why Monarch Butterflies Aren't Getting Endangered Species Status." *Smithsonian Magazine*, December 20, 2020. Accessed April 10, 2021, from https://www.smithsonianmag.com/smart-news/why-monarch-butterflies-arent-getting-endangered-species-status-180976586/.

Sharp, Ellen. "Mexico's Monarch Migration: Dealing with Deforestation in the Butterfly Forest." *Saving Earth Magazine*, Fall 2020. Accessed June 4, 2021, from https://issuu.com/savingearthmagazine/docs/saving_earth_magazine_fall_2020.

Sharp, Ellen. "Suspension of Flight." Terrain.org, April 7, 2022. Accessed May 24, 2022, from https://www.terrain.org/2022/nonfiction/suspension-of-flight/.

Sharp, Ellen, and Will Wright. "'We Were in Love with the Forest': Protecting Mexico's Monarch Butterfly Biosphere Reserve." *Forest History Today*, Spring /Fall 2020. Accessed June 4, 2021, from https://foresthistory.org/wp-content/uploads/2021/03/FHT-2020_Sharp_Wright_Protecting_Monarch_Butterflies.pdf.

Smith-Rodgers, Sheryl. "Maiden of the Monarchs: Discoverer of Butterfly Wintering Site Breaks Decades of Silence to Tell Her Story." *Texas Parks & Wildlife*, March 2016. Accessed November 17, 2019, from https://tpwmagazine.com/archive/2016/mar/LLL_catalina/.

St. Fleur, Nicholas. "Finding the Oldest Fossils of Butterflies Using a Human Nose Hair." *New York Times*, January 10, 2018. Accessed March 13, 2021, from https://www.nytimes.com/2018/01/10/science/fossils-butterflies-moths.html.

Urquhart, Fred A. "Found at Last: The Monarch's Winter Home." *National Geographic* 150, no. 2 (1976): 161–73.

Ward, Logan. "Top 10 Things to Know about the Day of the Dead." *National Geographic*, October 26, 2017. Accessed May 29, 2021, from https://www .nationalgeographic.com/travel/article/top-ten-day-of-dead-mexico.

Webster, Bayard. "2D Group Uncovers Butterflies' Secret." *New York Times*, May 29, 1977.

## NEWSLETTERS
Urquhart, Fred and Norah. *Insect Migration Studies* newsletter, vol. 1 (1964) to vol. 32 (1995). Available online in the Monarch Watch Reading Room at https:// monarchwatch.org/read/articles/.

## WEBSITES AND BLOGS
Anderson, Maria. "Five Facts about Día de los Muertos (The Day of the Dead)." *Smithsonian Stories* (blog), *Smithsonian*, October 30, 2016. Accessed May 29, 2021, from https://www.si.edu/stories/5-facts-about-dia-de-los-muertos-day-dead.

Bittel, Jason. "Monarch Butterflies Aren't Endangered, Reversing a Recent Decision. Is This Good News?" *National Geographic*, October 4, 2023. Accessed October 18, 2023. https://www.nationalgeographic.com/animals /article/migratory-monarch-butterflies-not-endangered-vulnerable.

Black, Scott. "Forests, Fires, and Insects." *Xerces Blog, Xerces Society*, December 19, 2020. Accessed October 1, 2022, from https://xerces.org/blog/forests -fires-and-insects.

Doncaster, C. Patrick. "Timeline of the Human Condition." April 5, 2021. Accessed April 6, 2021, from http://www.southampton.ac.uk/~cpd /history.html.

Frazer, Jennifer. "Butterflies in the Time of Dinosaurs, with Nary a Flower in Sight." *The Artful Amoeba* (blog), *Scientific American*, July 1, 2016. Accessed May 5, 2021, from https://blogs.scientificamerican.com/artful-amoeba /butterflies-in-the-time-of-dinosaurs-with-nary-a-flower-in-sight/.

Freeman, Dave. "Polar Explorer Will Steger: Still Testing the Limits." *Adventure* (blog), *National Geographic*, May 7, 2015. Accessed January 1, 2021, from https://www.nationalgeographic.com/adventure/article /polar-explorer-will-steger-still-testing-the-limits.

Galvez, Roberto, Stephen Gaylor, Charles Young, Nancy Patrick, Dexer Johnson, and Jose Ruiz. "The Space Shuttle and Its Operations." Accessed May 25, 2021, from https://www.nasa.gov/centers/johnson/pdf/584722main_Wings -ch3a-pgs53-73.pdf.

González-Duarte, Columba. "More Than Monarchs: Understanding Traditions Linked to Monarch Butterflies." Monarch Joint Venture, April 2, 2020. Accessed May 30, 2021, from https://monarchjointventure.org/blog/more -than-monarchs-understanding-traditions-linked-to-monarch-butterflies.

Governor General of Canada. "Order of Canada." Accessed March 6, 2020, from https://www.gg.ca/en/honours/canadian-honours/order-canada.

Hamline University. "Center for Global Environmental Education: CGEE's History," 2020. Retrieved January 1, 2021, from https://sites.google.com /hamline.edu/cgee/about-cgee/cgees-history.

Hancock, Lorin. "What Is Forest Degradation and Why Is It Bad for People and Wildlife?" World Wildlife Federation. Accessed May 22, 2021, from https://www.worldwildlife.org/stories/what-is-forest-degradation-and -why-is-it-bad-for-people-and-wildlife.

Howard, Elizabeth. "Exploring the Monarch's Winter Habitat in Mexico." Journey North. Accessed January 15, 2021, from https://journeynorth.org/tm /monarch/sl/34/article_sl.html.

Howard, Isis, and Emma Pelton. "Western Monarch Rebound to Final Tally of Nearly 250,000 Butterflies." Western Monarch Count, January 24, 2022. Accessed June 6, 2022, from https://www.westernmonarchcount .org/western-monarchs-rebound-to-final-tally-of-nearly-250000 -butterflies/.

Journey North. "How Do Monarchs Find Milkweed?" Accessed February 6, 2021, from https://journeynorth.org/tm/monarch/sl/30/text.html.

Lovett, Jim. "Monarch Population Status." *Monarch Watch Blog,* Monarch Watch, May 24, 2022. Accessed June 2, 2022, from https://monarchwatch.org /blog/2022/05/24/monarch-population-status-48/.

McKnight, Stephanie. "Monarch Numbers from Mexico Point to Declining Population." *Xerces Blog,* Xerces Society, February 26, 2021. Accessed May 5, 2021, from https://www.xerces.org/blog/monarch-numbers-from -mexico-point-to-declining-population.

Monarch Joint Venture. "Monarch Migration." 2021. Accessed May 5, 2021, from https://monarchjointventure.org/monarch-biology/monarch-migration.

Monarch Joint Venture. "Question and Answer: Do You Have Tips for Visiting the Overwintering Colonies in Mexico?" 2022. Accessed September 19, 2022, from https://monarchjointventure.org/faq/visiting-mexican-overwintering-sites.

Monarch Watch. "Biology: Monarch Life Cycle." Accessed February 22, 2020, from https://www.monarchwatch.org/biology/cycle1.htm.

Monarch Watch. "Dr. Fred Urquhart—In Memoriam." Accessed February 19, 2020, from https://www.monarchwatch.org/news/urquhart.htm.

NIH: National Human Genome Research Institute. "A Brief Guide to Genomics." Accessed April 6, 2021, from https://www.genome.gov/about-genomics/fact -sheets/A-Brief-Guide-to-Genomics.

Smithsonian's National Zoo & Conservation Biology Institute. "What Is Radio Telemetry?" Accessed November 14, 2020, from https://nationalzoo.si.edu /migratory-birds/what-radio-telemetry.

Taylor, Chip. "Monarch Numbers in Mexico: Predictions and Reality," *Monarch Watch Blog,* Monarch Watch, May 24, 2022. Accessed June 2, 2022, from https://monarchwatch.org/blog/2022/05/24/monarch-numbers-in-mexico -predictions-and-reality/.

UNESCO World Heritage Convention. "Monarch Butterfly Biosphere Reserve." 2021. Accessed May 21, 2021, from https://whc.unesco.org/en/list/1290/.

University of Minnesota College of Biological Sciences. "Frequently Asked Questions." 2015. Accessed February 22, 2020, from https://cbs.umn.edu /research/labs/lionresearch/faq.

Walker, A., K. S. Oberhauser, E. M. Pelton, J. M. Pleasants, and W. E. Thogmartin. 2022. "*Danaus plexippus* ssp. *plexippus. The IUCN Red List of Threatened Species* 2022: e.T194052138A200522253." Accessed September 29, 2022, from https://dx.doi.org/10.2305/IUCN.UK.2022-1.RLTS.T194052138A200522253.en.

Watt, Liz. "The Great Monarch Migration: A Unique Phenomenon Under Threat." World Wildlife Fund, March 16, 2021. Accessed May 21, 2021, from https://www.worldwildlife.org/stories/the-great-monarch-migration.

Western Monarch Count. "About." 2021. Accessed May 19, 2021, from https://www.westernmonarchcount.org/about/.

Wheeler, Justin. "Tropical Milkweed—A No-Grow." *Xerces Blog*, Xerces Society, April 19, 2018. Accessed May 21, 2021, from https://xerces.org/blog/tropical-milkweed-a-no-grow.

World Wildlife Fund. "Less Monarch Butterfly Presence and Increased Degradation in Its Hibernation Forests." February 25, 2021. Accessed May 21, 2021, from https://xerces.org/sites/default/files/publications/21-003.pdf.

World Wildlife Fund. "What Do Pandas Eat?" 2019. Accessed February 22, 2020, from https://wwf.panda.org/knowledge_hub/endangered_species/giant_panda/panda/what_do_pandas_they_eat/.

Xerces Society for Invertebrate Conservation. "Western Monarchs in Crisis." 2021. Accessed May 3, 2021, from https://xerces.org/western-monarch-call-to-action.

## PODCASTS

Castello y Tickell, Sofia, and Julia Migne. "Activism and Ecopoetry with Homero Aridjis." Produced by the University of Oxford. *Good Natured*. November 3, 2020. Podcast, 29:17. https://podcasts.ox.ac.uk/activism-and-ecopoetry-homero-aridjis.

Gwin, Peter. "Searching for a Butterfly in a Conflict Zone: A Photographer Searches for an Elusive Butterfly to Help Reconnect with Her Late Father." Produced by National Geographic. *Overheard*. Episode 34. September 20, 2022. Podcast, 28:19. https://www.nationalgeographic.com/podcasts/article/episode-34-searching-for-a-butterfly-in-a-conflict-zone.

Yaquinto, Jessica, and Lyle Balenquah. "Convergent Migrations of Humans and Monarch Butterflies." Archaeology Podcast Network. *Heritage Voices*. Episode 44. Podcast, 1:00:00. https://www.columbagonzalez.com/post /penne-allarrabbiata.

## INTERVIEWS AND CORRESPONDENCE

Agrawal, Anurag; email message to Dana L. Church, February 24, 2020.

Fisher, Kelsey E.; personal interview, February 13, 2020.

Forest History Society. Comisíon Estatal de Parques Naturales y de la Fauna (CEPANAF) Oral History Interviews, 2020. Accessed January 27, 2023, from https://foresthistory.org/research-explore/archives-library/fhs-archival -collections/cepanaf-mexico-oral-history-interviews/.

González-Duarte, Columba; personal interview, June 17, 2021.

Howard, Elizabeth; personal interview, December 8, 2020.

Howard, Isis; email message to Dana L. Church, September 27, 2022.

Jepsen, Sarina; email message to Dana L. Church, September 28, 2022.

Leong, Kingston L. H.; email message to Dana L. Church, April 28, 2021.

Malcolm, Stephen B.; email message to Dana L. Church, September 28, 2020.

Monroe, Mía; email message to Dana L. Church, May 16, 2021.

Oberhauser, Karen; email message to Dana L. Church, February 1, 2021.

Prysby, Michelle; personal interview, April 7, 2021.

Taylor, Orley R.; email message to Dana L. Church, January 27, 2020.

Taylor, Orley R.; email message to Dana L. Church, November 18, 2020.

Urquhart, Fred A.; interview by Paul A. Bader [recording]. University of Toronto Archives Oral History Project. University of Toronto Archives, Toronto, Canada. January 11, 1979.

Wright, Will; telephone conversation with Dana L. Church, January 27, 2023.

## VIDEOS AND PRESENTATIONS

AustinButterflies.org. "Grand Saga of the Monarch Butterfly Lecture by Lincoln P. Brower," YouTube, 1:04:32, March 24, 2014. Accessed August 2, 2021, from https://www.youtube.com/watch?v=DXfADznFAZ4.

AustinButterflies.org. "Discovery of the Monarch's Mexican Overwintering Refugia by Catalina Aguado, John Christian, Bill Calvert, and Lincoln Brower," YouTube, 1:42:20, May 1, 2014. Accessed August 2, 2021, from https://www.youtube.com/watch?v=3TBu5YLv7CI.

Brower, Lincoln P., and Jonathan C. Huberth. "Strategy for Survival: Behavioral Ecology of the Monarch Butterfly," YouTube, 29:38, March 28, 2013. Accessed August 2, 2021, from https://www.youtube.com/watch?v=Qkq_ZZGFPjM.

González-Duarte, Columba. "Love and Disgust: One Butterfly Two Worlds." April 13, 2021. Accessed June 10, 2021, from https://www.columbagonzalez.com/post/love-and-disgust-one-butterfly-two-worlds. (Seminar given April 7, 2021, for the Heroes and Villains in the Anthropocene, Brunel University, London.)

## REPORTS

Henderson, A. M., J. A. Gervais, B. Luukinen, K. Buhl, K. D. Stone, A. Cross, and J. Jenkins. *Glyphosate General Fact Sheet*. 2010. National Pesticide Information Center, Oregon State University Extension Services. Accessed May 25, 2021, from http://npic.orst.edu/factsheets/glyphogen.html.

US Department of Agriculture, Economic Research Service. "U.S. Avocado Demand Is Climbing Steadily." March 20, 2020. Accessed June 29, 2021, from https://www.ers.usda.gov/data-products/chart-gallery/gallery/chart-detail/?chartId=98071.

US Department of the Interior, Fish and Wildlife Service, "Endangered and Threatened Wildlife and Plants; 12-Month Finding for the Monarch Butterfly," *Federal Register* 85, no. 243 (December 17, 2020): 81813. Accessed April 10, 2021, from https://www.govinfo.gov/content/pkg/FR-2020-12-17/pdf/2020-27523.pdf.

## DISSERTATIONS

Hitchcock, Colleen Brandes. "Survival of Caterpillars in the Face of Predation by Birds: Predator-Free Space, Caterpillar Mimicry, and Protective Coloration." PhD diss., University of Pennsylvania, 2004. ProQuest 3152052.

## SCIENTIFIC JOURNAL ARTICLES

Anderson, J. B., and L. P. Brower. "Freeze-Protection of Overwintering Monarch Butterflies in Mexico: Critical Role of the Forest as a Blanket and an Umbrella." *Ecological Entomology* 21 (1996): 107–16.

Arikawa, Kentaro, and Kiyoshi Aoki. "Response Characteristics and Occurrence of Extraocular Photoreceptors on Lepidopteran Genitalia." *Journal of Comparative Physiology A* 148 (1982): 483–89. https://doi.org/10.1007/BF00619786.

Blackiston, Douglas, Adriana D. Briscoe, and Martha R. Weiss. "Color Vision and Learning in the Monarch Butterfly, *Danaus plexippus* (Nymphalidae)." *Journal of Experimental Biology* 214 (2011): 509–20. https://doi.org/10.1242/jeb.048728.

Brower, Lincoln P. "Understanding and Misunderstanding the Migration of the Monarch Butterfly (Nymphalidae) in North America: 1857–1995." *Journal of the Lepidopterists' Society* 49, no. 4 (1995): 304–85.

Brower, Lincoln P., and William H. Calvert. "Foraging Dynamics of Bird Predators on Overwintering Monarch Butterflies in Mexico." *Evolution* 39, no. 4 (1985): 852–68.

Brower, Lincoln P., Howard B. Horner, Melanie A. Marty, Christine M. Moffitt, and Bernardo Villa-R. "Mice (*Peromyscus maniculatus, P. spicilegus, and Microtus mexicanus*) as Predators of Overwintering Monarch Butterflies (*Danaus plexippus*) in Mexico." *Biotropica* 17, no. 2 (1985): 89–99.

Brower, Lincoln P., Jane Van Zandt Brower, and Joseph M. Corvino. "Plant Poisons in a Terrestrial Food Chain." *Proceedings of the National Academy of Science of the United States of America* 57 (1967): 893–98.

Brower, Lincoln P., Ernest H. Williams, Linda S. Fink, Daniel A. Slayback, Isabel M. Ramírez, M. Ván Limón García, and Raúl R. Zubieta. "Overwintering Clusters of the Monarch Butterfly Coincide with the Least Hazardous Vertical Temperatures in the Oyamel Forest." *Journal of the Lepidopterists' Society* 65, no. 1 (2011): 27–46.

Brower, Lincoln P., Ernest H. Williams, Daniel A. Slayback, Linda S. Fink, Isabel M. Ramírez, Raúl R. Zubieta, M. Ivan Limon Garcia, Paul Gier, Jennifer A. Lear, and Tonya Van Hook. "Oyamel Fir Forest Trunks Provide Thermal Advantages for Overwintering Monarch Butterflies in Mexico." *Insect Conservation and Diversity* 2 (2009): 163–75.

Calvert, William H., Willow Zuchowski, and Lincoln P. Brower. "The Effect of Rain, Snow and Freezing Temperatures on Overwintering Monarch Butterflies in Mexico." *Biotropica* 15, no. 1 (1983): 42–47.

Cepero, Laurel C., Laura C. Rosenwald, and Martha R. Weiss. "The Relative Importance of Flower Color and Shape for the Foraging Monarch Butterfly (Lepidoptera: Nymphalidae)." *Journal of Insect Behavior* 28 (2015): 499–511. https://doi.org/10.1007/s10905-015-9519-z.

Clarke, Anthony R., and Myron P. Zalucki. "Monarchs in Australia: On the Winds of a Storm?" *Biological Invasions* 6 (2004): 123–27.

Fink, Linda S., and Lincoln P. Brower. "Birds Can Overcome the Cardenolide Defence of Monarch Butterflies in Mexico." *Nature* 291 (1981): 67–70.

Fisher, Kelsey E., James S. Adelman, and Steven P. Bradbury. "Employing Very High Frequency (VHF) Radio Telemetry to Recreate Monarch Butterfly Flight Paths." *Environmental Entomology* 49, no. 2 (March 2020): 312–23. https://doi.org/10.1093/ee/nvaa019.

Flores-Martínez, José Juan, Anuar Martínez-Pacheco, Eduardo Rendón-Salinas, Jorge Rickards, Sahotra Sarkar, and Victor Sánchez-Cordero. "Recent Forest Cover Loss in the Core Zones of the Monarch Butterfly Biosphere Reserve in Mexico." *Frontiers in Environmental Science* 7 (2019): article no. 167. https://doi.org/10.3389/fenvs.2019.00167.

Flores-Martínez, José Juan, Eduardo Rendón-Salinas, Anuar Martínez-Pacheco, Rubén Salinas-Galicia, Mariana Munguía-Carrara, Jorge Rickards, Sahotra Sarkar, and Víctor Sánchez-Cordero. "Policy Implementation Halts Deforestation in Winter Habitat of Monarch Butterflies in Mexico." *BioScience* 70, no. 6 (2020): 449–51. https://doi.org/10.1093/biosci/biaa038.

Freedman, Micah G., Jacobus C. de Roode, Matthew Forister, Marcus R. Kronforst, Amanda A. Pierce, Cheryl B. Schultz, Orley R. Taylor, and Elizabeth E. Crone. "Are Eastern and Western Monarch Butterflies Distinct Populations? A Review of Evidence for Ecological, Phenotypic, and Genetic

Differentiation and Implications for Conservation." *Conservation Science and Practice* (early view) (2021): e432. https://doi.org/10.1111/csp2.432.

González-Duarte, Columba. "Butterflies, Organized Crime, and 'Sad Trees': A Critique of the Monarch Butterfly Biosphere Reserve Program in a Context of Rural Violence." *World Development* 142 (2021): 105420. https://doi.org /10.1016/j.worlddev.2021.105420.

Guerra, Patrick A., Robert J. Gegear, and Steven M. Reppert. "A Magnetic Compass Aids Monarch Butterfly Migration." *Nature Communications* 5 (2014): 4164. https://doi.org/10.1038/ncomms5164.

Haribal, Meena, and J. A. A. Renwick. "Differential Postalightment Oviposition Behavior of Monarch Butterflies on *Asclepias* Species." *Journal of Insect Behavior* 11, no. 4 (1998): 507–38.

Howard, Elizabeth, and Andrew K. Davis. "The Fall Migration Flyways of Monarch Butterflies in Eastern North America Revealed by Citizen Scientists." *Journal of Insect Conservation* 13 (2009): 279–86. https://doi.org /10.1007/s10841-008-9169-y.

Howard, Elizabeth, and Andrew K. Davis. "Investigating Long-Term Changes in the Spring Migration of Monarch Butterflies (Lepidoptera: Nymphalidae) Using 18 Years of Data from Journey North, a Citizen Science Program." *Annals of the Entomological Society of America* 108, no. 5 (2015): 664–69. https://doi.org/10.1093/aesa/sav061.

Kutz, Susan, and Matilde Tomaselli. "'Two-Eyed Seeing' Supports Wildlife Health." *Science* 364, no. 6446 (2019): 1135–37. https://doi.org/10.1126 /science.aau6170.

Labandeira, Conrad C., Qiang Yang, Jorge A. Santiago-Blay, Carol L. Hotton, Antónia Monteiro, Yong-Jie Wang, Yulia Goreva, ChungKun Shih, Sandra Siljeström, Tim R. Rose, David L. Dilcher, and Dong Ren. "The Evolutionary Convergence of Mid-Mesozoic Lacewings and Cenozoic Butterflies." *Proceedings of the Royal Society B* 283 (2016): 20152893. https://doi.org/10.1098/rspb.2015.2893.

Leong, Kingston L. H., Robert Dees, Holly Sletteland, Josh Heptig, Judy Richards, and Judy Reina. "The Seasonal Occupancy of Overwintering Monarch Butterflies, *Danaus plexippus plexippus* (Linnaeus, 1758)

(Lepidoptera: Nymphalidae), at Four California Winter Groves Reflects Conditions for Winter Aggregations, Survival, and Contribution to the Next Generation of Butterflies." *Pan-Pacific Entomologist* 96, no. 2 (2020): 41–58.

Lohmann, K. J., P. Luschi, and G. C. Hays. "Goal Navigation and Island-Finding in Sea Turtles." *Journal of Experimental Marine Biology and Ecology* 356, nos. 1 & 2 (2008): 83–95. https://doi.org/10.1016/j.jembe.2007.12.017.

Merlin, Christine, Robert J. Gegear, and Steven M. Reppert. "Antennal Circadian Clocks Coordinate Sun Compass Orientation in Migratory Monarch Butterflies." *Science* 325, no. 5948 (2009): 1700–4. https://doi.org/10.1126/science.1176221.

Monasterio, Fernando Ortíz, Vicente Sánchez, Hugo González Liquidano, and Marta Venegas. "Magnetism as a Complementary Factor to Explain Orientation Systems Used by Monarch Butterflies to Locate Their Overwintering Areas." *Atala: Journal of the Xerces Society* 9, nos. 1 & 2 (1981–84): 14–16. https://www.biodiversitylibrary.org/item/235405.

Mouritsen, Henrik, and Barrie J. Frost. "Virtual Migration in Tethered Flying Monarch Butterflies Reveals Their Orientation Mechanisms." *Proceedings of the National Academy of Sciences* 99, no. 15 (2002): 10162–66. https://doi.org/10.1073/pnas.152137299.

Nail, Kelly R., Lara Drizd, and Kristen J. Voorhies. "Butterflies across the Globe: A Synthesis of the Current Status and Characteristics of Monarch (*Danaus plexippus*) Populations Worldwide." *Frontiers in Ecology and Evolution* 7 (2019): 362. https://doi.org/10.3389/fevo.2019.00362.

Oberhauser, Karen S., Alfonso Alonso, Stephen B. Malcolm, Ernest H. Williams, and Myron P. Zalucki. "Lincoln Brower, Champion for Monarchs." *Frontiers in Ecology and Evolution* 7 (2019): 149. https://doi.org/10.3389/fevo.2019.00149.

Ogarrio, Rodolfo. "Development of the Civic Group, Pro Monarca, A. C., for the Protection of the Monarch Butterfly Wintering Grounds in the Republic of Mexico." *Atala: Journal of the Xerces Society* 9, nos. 1 & 2 (1981–84): 11–13. https://www.biodiversitylibrary.org/item/235405.

Pelton, Emma M., Cheryl B. Schultz, Sarina J. Jepsen, Scott Hoffman Black, and Elizabeth E. Crone. "Western Monarch Population Plummets: Status, Probable Causes, and Recommended Conservation Actions." *Frontiers in Ecology and Evolution* 7 (2019): 258. https://doi.org/10.3389 /fevo.2019.00258.

Pelling, Andrew E., Paul R. Wilkinson, Richard Stringer, and James K. Gimzewski. "Dynamic Mechanical Oscillations during Metamorphosis of the Monarch Butterfly." *Journal of the Royal Society Interface* 6 (2009): 29–37. https://doi .org/10.1098/rsif.2008.0224.

Reid, Andrea J., Lauren E. Eckert, John-Francis Lane, Nathan Young, Scott G. Hinch, Chris T. Darimont, Steven J. Cooke, Natalie C. Ban, and Albert Marshall. "'Two-Eyed Seeing': An Indigenous Framework to Transform Fisheries Research and Management." *Fish and Fisheries* 22, no. 2 (2021): 243–61. https://doi.org/10.1111/faf.12516.

Reppert, Steven M., and Jacobus C. de Roode. "Demystifying Monarch Butterfly Migration." *Current Biology* 28, no. 17 (2018): R1009–R1022. https://doi .org/10.1016/j.cub.2018.02.067.

Reppert, Steven M., Patrick A. Guerra, and Christine Merlin. "Neurobiology of Monarch Butterfly Migration." *Annual Review of Entomology* 61 (2016): 25– 42. http://doi.org/10.1146/annurev-ento-010814-020855.

Rodrigues, Daniela, Brad W. Goodner, and Martha R. Weiss. "Reversal Learning and Risk-Averse Foraging Behavior in the Monarch Butterfly, *Danaus plexippus* (Lepidoptera: Nymphalidae)." *Ethology* 116, no. 3 (2010): 270–80. https://doi.org/10.1111/j.1439-0310.2009.01737.x.

Rothschild, Miriam, and Gunnar Bergström. "The Monarch Butterfly Caterpillar (*Danaus plexippus*) Waves at Passing Hymenoptera and Jet Aircraft—Are Repellent Volatiles Released Simultaneously?" *Phytochemistry* 45, no. 6 (1997): 1139–44.

Sohn, Jae-Cheon, Conrad C. Labandeira, and Donald R. Davis. "The Fossil Record and Taphonomy of Butterflies and Moths (Insecta, Lepidoptera): Implications for Evolutionary Diversity and Divergence-Time Estimates." *BMC Evolutionary Biology* 15 (2015): 12–27. https://doi.org/10.1186 /s12862-015-0290-8.

Stenoien, Carl, Kelly R. Nail, and Karen S. Oberhauser. "Habitat Productivity and Temporal Patterns of Monarch Butterfly Egg Densities in the Eastern United States." *Annals of the Entomological Society of America* 108, no. 5 (2015): 670–79. https://doi.org/10.1093/aesa/sav054.

Stenoien, Carl, Kelly R. Nail, Jacinta M. Zalucki, Hazel Parry, Karen S. Oberhauser, and Myron P. Zalucki. "Monarchs in Decline: A Collateral Landscape-Level Effect of Modern Agriculture." *Insect Science* 25, no. 4 (2018): 528–41. https://doi.org/10.1111/1744-7917.12404.

Stringer, Richard P. "Watching the Inside of a Maturing Monarch Chrysalis Using MRI." *Metamorphosis* 11, no. 3 (2000): 132–45.

Taylor, Chantel J., and Jayne E. Yack. "Hearing in Caterpillars of the Monarch Butterfly (*Danaus plexippus*)." *Journal of Experimental Biology* 222, no. 22 (2019): jeb211862. https://doi.org/10.1242/jeb.211862.

Taylor, Orley R. Jr., James P. Lovett, David L. Gibo, Emily L. Weiser, Wayne E. Thogmartin, Darius J. Semmens, James E. Diffendorfer, John M. Pleasants, Samuel D. Pecoraro, and Ralph Grundel. "Is the Timing, Pace, and Success of the Monarch Migration Associated with Sun Angle?" *Frontiers in Ecology and Evolution* 7, article 442 (2019): 1–15. https://doi.org/10.3389/fevo.2019.00442.

Taylor, Orley R. Jr., John M. Pleasants, Ralph Grundel, Samuel D. Pecoraro, James P. Lovett, and Ann Ryan. "Evaluating the Migration Mortality Hypothesis Using Monarch Tagging Data." *Frontiers in Ecology and Evolution* 8, article 264 (2020): 1–13. https://doi.org/10.3389/fevo.2020.00264.

Tracy, James L., Tuula Kantola, Kristen A. Baum, and Robert N. Coulson. "Modeling Fall Migration Pathways and Spatially Identifying Potential Migratory Hazards for the Eastern Monarch Butterfly." *Landscape Ecology* 34 (2019): 443–58. https://doi.org/10.1007/s10980-019-00776-0.

Urquhart, F. A. "Monarch Butterfly (*Danaus plexippus*) Migrations Studies: Autumnal Movement." *Proceedings of the Entomological Society of Ontario* 95 (1964): 23–33.

Urquhart, Fred A., and Norah R. Urquhart. "The Overwintering Site of the Eastern Population of the Monarch Butterfly (*Danaus P. Plexippus; Danaidae*) in Southern Mexico." *Journal of the Lepidopterists' Society* 30, no. 3 (1976): 153–58.

van Eldijk, Timo J. B., Torsten Wappler, Paul K. Strother, Carolien M. H. van der Weijst, Hossein Rajaei, Henk Visscher, and Bas van de Schootbrugge. "A Triassic-Jurassic Window into the Evolution of Lepidoptera." *Science Advances* 4 (2018): e1701568. https://doi.org/10.1126/sciadv.1701568.

van Emden, Helmut F., and Sir John Gurdon. "Dame Miriam Louisa Rothchild CBE." *Biographical Memoirs of the Fellows of the Royal Society* 52 (January 2005): 315–30.

Yang, Qiang, Yongjie Wang, Conrad C. Labandeira, Chungkun Shih, and Dong Ren. "Mesozoic Lacewings from China Provide Phylogenetic Insight into Evolution of the Kalligrammatidae (Neuroptera)." *BMC Evolutionary Biology* 14 (2014): 126–56. https://doi.org/10.1186/1471-2148-14-126.

Zalucki, M. P., L. P. Brower, and S. B. Malcolm. "Oviposition by *Danaus plexippus* in Relation to Cardenolide Content of Three *Asclepias* Species in the Southeastern U.S.A." *Ecological Entomology* 15, no. 2 (1990): 231–40.

Zhan, Shuai, Wei Zhang, Kristjan Niitepõld, Jeremy Hsu, Juan Fernández Haeger, Myron P. Zalucki, Sonia Altizer, Jacobus C. de Roode, Steven M. Reppert, and Marcus Kronforst. "The Genetics of Monarch Butterfly Migration and Warning Colouration." *Nature* 514 (2014): 317–21. https://doi.org/10.1038/nature13812.

Zylstra, Erin R., Leslie Ries, Naresh Neupane, Sarah P. Saunders, M. Isabel Ramírez, Eduardo Rendón-Salinas, Karen S. Oberhauser, Matthew T. Farr, and Elise F. Zipkin. "Changes in Climate Drive Recent Monarch Butterfly Dynamics." *Nature Ecology & Evolution* 5 (2021): 1441–52. https://doi.org/10.1038/s41559-021-01504-1.

# PHOTO CREDITS

# ACKNOWLEDGMENTS

A few years ago, my agent mentioned on social media that she wished someone would write a book about butterflies. The topic seemed too big for me, but I thought I could perhaps narrow it down. I always liked monarch butterflies, so I did a bit of research. I was quickly hooked. So a huge thank-you goes to my wonderful agent, Stacey Kondla, for the inspiration behind this book. Most of all, I thank Stacey for her unwavering support and dedication, and for being an overall awesome human being.

To Lisa Sandell at Scholastic: Thank you for believing in me.

To my editor, Jody Corbett: I am immensely grateful that you accompanied me on this journey. Thank you for being my guide, for sharing your incredible expertise, for your enthusiasm, for your keen eye, and for teaching me so much. I truly feel as though this manuscript—and myself as a writer—underwent a metamorphosis since I began working with you.

Many thanks to Maeve Norton, Lisa Broderick, Kassy Lopez, and Emily Theresa at Scholastic, who helped bring this book to life, with additional thanks to Cian O'Day for photo research and Joy Simpkins for copyediting. Thank you to everyone else at Scholastic for their support: Ellie Berger, David Levithan, Erin Berger, Seale Ballenger, Amanda Trautmann, Lizette Serrano, Emily Heddleson, Sabrina Montenigro, Maisha Johnson, Meredith Wardell, Rachel Feld, Katie Dutton, Kelsey Albertson, Holly Alexander, Julie Beckman, Tracy Bozentka, Savanah D'Amico, Barbara Holloway, Sarah Herbik, Roz Hilden, Brigid Martin, Liz Morici, Dan Moser, Nikki Mutch, Sydney Niegos, Caroline Noll, Debby Owusu-Appiah, Bob Pape, Jacqueline Perumal, Betsy Politi, Jacquelyn Rubin, Chris Satterlund, Terribeth Smith, Jody Stigliano, Sarah Sullivan, Melanie Wann, Jarad Waxman, and Elizabeth Whiting.

Much gratitude goes to all the scientists and monarch butterfly advocates I featured in this book, and who kindly answered my numerous questions and helped me get my facts straight: Dr. Anurag Agrawal, Dr. Kelsey Fisher, Dr. Columba González-Duarte, Dr. Meena Haribal, Elizabeth Howard, Isis Howard, Sarina Jepsen, Dr. Kingston Leong, Mía Monroe, Dr. Stephen Malcolm, Dr. Karen Oberhauser, Michelle Prysby, Dr.

Steven M. Reppert, and Dr. Orley (Chip) Taylor. To all these individuals and their research teams: Thank you for all of the important work you do. Any remaining errors in this book are mine and mine alone.

A special thank-you to the librarians who worked their magic to help me find what I was looking for: Marnee Gamble, University of Toronto Archives; Tanis Franco, University of Toronto Scarborough Library; and Tom Harding, University of Waterloo Library. Thank you also to my local libraries, the University of Waterloo Library, the Kitchener Public Library, and the Waterloo Public Library.

To Catalina Trail and Sheryl Smith-Rodgers: Thank you for sharing Catalina's incredible story. I am so glad her voice is finally being heard.

My heartfelt thanks to Celso Mendoza and Dr. Will Wright, for taking the time to read the entire manuscript with an eye toward cultural and historical accuracy. Again, any lingering errors in this book are mine.

To Barbara Kingsolver, who gave me a boost when I needed it.

Cia Penner has been my constant source of encouragement and support ever since I was a student in her high school biology class. Thank you, Cia, from the bottom of my heart, for always being there, for reading countless drafts, for your friendship, for helping me navigate life's many challenges, and for celebrating my accomplishments, big and small.

To Stephen, Lelynd, and Lexi: Thank you for your love and support, for playing along while I chased butterflies, and for listening patiently every time I talked about butterflies during dinnertime conversations. I am pleased that you now have a deeper appreciation for monarch butterflies, too.

And finally, to the monarch butterflies. While I was writing this book, the world experienced the COVID-19 pandemic and I lost beloved family members. During those challenging times, your resilience and beauty were a source of inspiration to me. You also had a knack for appearing in our garden or during a walk at just the right time, giving my spirits the lift they needed. Thank you for sparking wonder, awe, and hope in people around the world. This book is my humble way of giving back, and hopefully it will inspire others to give back to you as well.

# INDEX

Note: Page numbers in *italics* refer to illustrations, tables, or graphs.

eggs of monarchs
    chorion of, 3
    close-up view of, *4*
    density of, 128
    development in, 3
    females laying, 8, 24, 102, 127, 160,
        162, 163, 213
    research on, 124, 125–29
    size of, 3
Eisner, Tom, 157
ejidatarios, 232–33, 267
ejidos
    decision-making powers of, 236, 243
    definition of, 56, 267
    ejidatarios as leaders of, 232–33, 267
    forests managed by, 56
    in Monarch Biosphere, 207–8, 211
    rights of, 56
Endangered Species Act, 178, 184, 196,
    205
entomology, 130, 267
ethnography, 225, 226, 267
Etuaptmumk, 251
eucalyptus trees, 193–94, 205, *206*
exoskeletons of butterflies, 78, 268
eyes, of monarchs, 19, 150, 157, 163–64
eyespots, *170*, 171

F
farming. *See* agriculture
female monarchs
    characteristics of, *25*
    laying eggs, 8, 24, 102, 127, 160, 162,
        163, 213
    and milkweed plants, 127–28, 156–63
    shrinking breeding area for, 102
Fisher, Kelsey, 129–41, 213
flavonoids, 163, 268

flies, 5, 12
*Flight of the Butterflies* (film), 55
flight patterns of monarchs, 130–42
flight simulators, 145–51, *146*, 153–54
flowers. *See* nectar; wildflowers
flyways, 117, 120–22
forest degradation, 212, 267
fossils, 169–74, *170*
frass, 17, 268
freezing (defense mechanism), 12
Frost, Barrie J., 145–47

G
García, Leonila Vázquez, 207, 236
genomics, 175, 268
genomic techniques, 175, 176, 183,
    268
glyphosate, 103–4, 268
glyphosate-resistant plants, 103
González-Duarte, Columba
    on acting locally, 249
    on blaming countries, 247–49
    on conservation challenges, 248–49
    education of, 224–25
    ethnographic studies of Monarch
        Biosphere by, 225–26, 230, 236,
        238–39
    on "heroes vs. villains" theme, 246–47
    on Indigenous knowledge, 241–44
    on PES system, 232, 233
    on resilience of monarchs, 249–50
green milkweed (*Asclepias viridis*), 66, 92
greenness, 107
grosbeaks, black-headed, 77, 78
groves, 193–94, 195, 268
Grupo de los Cien, 222, 240
guardabosques, 61, 268
gymnosperms, 171–72, 267, 268

# ABOUT THE AUTHOR

Dana L. Church is the author of *The Beekeepers: How Humans Changed the World of Bumble Bees* and *Animal Minds: What Are They Thinking?* She studied bumble bees for her PhD at the University of Ottawa, Canada (and was never stung!). She lives in southern Ontario with her husband, their two children, and their big, black, friendly dog.

You can find out more about Dana and her writing at danachurchwriter.com.